TR(

OUTLIVES

THE LIE

7 Steps to Overcoming the Spirit of Accusation

DR. VICTORIA DUNSTON

TRILOGY
PROFESSIONAL PUBLISHING MEETS POWERFUL PROMOTION
A wholly owned subsidiary of TBN

Trilogy Christian Publishers
A Wholly Owned Subsidiary of Trinity Broadcasting Network
2442 Michelle Drive
Tustin, CA 92780

Truth Outlives the Lie

For information, address Trilogy Christian Publishing
Rights Department, 2442 Michelle Drive, Tustin, Ca 92780.
Trilogy Christian Publishing/ TBN and colophon are trademarks of Trinity Broadcasting Network.
For information about special discounts for bulk purchases, please contact Trilogy Christian Publishing.
Manufactured in the United States of America

This book is a work of non-fiction. Although portions of this book are derived from real events, each character in it is fictional, a composite drawing from several individuals and from imagination. No reference to any living or deceased person is intended or should be inferred.

Unless otherwise indicated, all scripture quotations marked (KJV) are from the King James Version of the Bible; New King James Version (NKJV); Easy-to-Read Version (ERV); New International Version (NIV); Revised Standard Version (RSV); or Christian Standard Bible (CSB).

Contact information:
Phone: (407) 325-5103
Email: nspiredwoman@gmail.com
Website: http://www.drivctoriadunston.com ISBN: insert here [Ex: 123-456-7890-0]

First Edition

Manufactured in the United States of America

10 9 8 7 6 5 4 3 2 1
Library of Congress Cataloging-in-Publication Data is available.
ISBN 978-1-63769-364-3
ISBN 978-1-63769-365-0 (ebook)

CONTENTS

"Vindicate me in your righteousness,
Lord my God; do not let them
gloat over me" Psalm 35:24 (NIV).

FOREWORD by Apostle Kimberly Daniels

Kimberly has several books that are listed as top twenty best sellers in the African American market. She was named one of the 70 Christian African American History Makers for 2013. She also has 49 commentaries in the Spiritual Warfare Bible. She is a renown American minister, Christian author, politician, and mother of four from Jacksonville, Florida. She served on the Jacksonville City Council and as the representative for Florida House of Representatives District 14.

There are countless numbers of people that have been affected by the spirit of accusation. A book with step-by-step instructions on how to overcome this force is needed. The enemy is constantly accusing us to God in order to hinder breakthroughs and manifestations, but when we recognize who we are and what has been done for us through the blood of Jesus we will rise above it. Every person that has accepted Jesus Christ as Lord has rights and ignorance is a tool that is used to take advantage of them.

Ephesians 6:12 For we wrestle not against flesh and blood, but against principalities, against powers, against the rulers of the darkness of this world, against spiritual wickedness in high places. We recognize that that the enemy is the culprit, but he works through human beings to try to get us to focus on that which is a distraction. As you make a conscious decision to recognize the enemy and push past the distraction of accusation, you will begin to soar in new realms of spirituality.

In this book, Dr. Victoria shares insights as to how many people in scripture were accused, both the guilty and the innocent, demonstrating that is possible to overcome the devastation of accusation. Yet repeatedly you will see how this force came against them and they lived to overcome it and master it.

With the Apostle Paul we see on many occasions this force would revolt against him simply for obeying the instructions God had given him. Many of you reading right now are targeted by this force and it has followed you all your life. It is time for it to break and you to recover from its effects on your life.

As you read this book and apply its principles you will discover that you had everything you needed all along. Now you must enforce your authority, using the Word of God, overcome and share your testimonies with others.

Purpose in your heart that you will not be a victim of accusation or any other demonic force that comes to delay your destiny. Rise and move with precision and make a deposit in the earth that will affect generations after you.

This book is an easy read, easy to understand, power pack that will serve as a guide to help you continuously walk in victory over accusation. You will want to read it repeatedly as a refresher.

Victoria Dunston is a woman of God, that loves the Lord with a tremendous gift to write and heart to serve God's people. The pages of this book is filled with her desire to provide the reader with applicable tools that enable them to walk continuously free.

My Apostle, John Eckhardt, always told me that the best thing a person could do to add to their legacy is to write a book. This book surely makes a statement that will forever rule over her generations. The Spirit of the scribe came upon her as she penned these pages of truth. I'm proud to know her and can't wait to get my copy.

Apostle Kimberly Daniels

Forward by Dr. Edward A. Addison

Dr Edward Akinlolu Addison has been a Pastor/teacher for over 25 years. He started his first fellowship at the University of Ibadan over 35 years ago, whilst in medical school. He has since gone on to pioneer and plant other churches in the UK. He currently spends his time in his apostolic calling travelling extensively to the nations: India, America Caribbean's and within Europe. Outside of Ministry Pastor Edward brings his considerable master's in theology, and bachelor's in biblical studies to use as a Social-Entrepreneur. He has served as a consultant for Government organisations, has been a panel member on the BBC and run a weekly programme on Premier radio. He also held community consultancy around gun and knife crime in young black men as a consultant of the former mayor of London, Boris Johnson.

Dr. Victoria Dunston in this exciting and seminal book, *Truth Outlives The Lie,* intricately weaves together a tapestry of her experience with Scripture to convey poignant lessons that will be of immense encouragement to anyone who has been a victim of offensive and callous actions or words. Her lengthy and valuable experience as a minister of Christ who has served both as a Pastor and a conference minister echoes through her words. Her passion and heart to see people whole and healed speak for itself through her writing.

She takes you expertly through a journey of some of the main figures of the Bible and draws out nuggets of truth that make you realise that you are not alone in dealing with unhealthy relationships. All of us at some point in time past and present have been in bewildering situations where offences have come our way from those we least expect and this has left us angry, shocked and shaken. Victoria draws out vital and valuable lessons for those who are hurting.

Truth Outlives The Lie, provides you with a toolbox to come out of those situations transformed rather than toxic. Pick it up, read it and apply the life lessons that this book provides for you.

Dr Edward A. Addison B.Th M.Th; Litt.D. FInstLM

Introduction

"Sticks and Stones May Break My Bones,
but Words Can Break My Spirit."

- Dr. Victoria Dunston

Many people's lives have been destroyed because of the words that have been spoken against them, and in some cases they were lies, exaggerations, and partial truths. In life we have all had situations and words spoken against us that were filled with false accusations, and if we are honest with ourselves, those words cut deeper than we care to think. Sadly, people tend to judge us based on those slanderous statements. It is wrong. It is painful. It can be heartbreaking; however, you will overcome.

Firstly, let me say, if this is happening to you and you are in a season of hurt and pain, I apologize that you have had to go through this. I'd also like to remind you that you will overcome!

1 John 5:4 (NKJV)

For whatever is born of God overcomes the world. And this is the victory that has overcome the world-our faith.

Surprisingly, you may be unaware that the person who comes to attack you is not your enemy. Satan is the accuser of the brethren, and you must realize that; otherwise, you may find yourself fighting a battle you cannot possibly win. There are deep forces that you cannot see operating through individuals, and God is exposing them in this season. Satan is an expert at fighting a carnal fight, with a highly strategic army that will never break rank.

Ephesians 6:12 (NKJV)

For we do not wrestle against flesh and blood, but against principalities, against powers, against the rulers of the darkness of this age, against spiritual hosts of wickedness in the heavenly places.

You are being accused day and night by your real enemy.

Revelation 12:9-11 (KJV)

⁹And the great dragon was cast out, that old serpent, called the Devil, and Satan, which deceiveth the whole world: he was cast out into the earth, and his angels were cast out with him. ¹⁰And I heard a loud voice saying in heaven, Now is come salvation, and strength, and the kingdom of our God, and the power of his Christ: for the accuser of our brethren is cast down, which accused them before our God day and night. ¹¹And they overcame him by the blood of the Lamb, and by the word of their testimony; and they loved not their lives unto the death.

You will be given tools that will help you see the real enemy behind the painful lies and accusations you may be facing. You will also realize that these people who have allowed the enemy to use them are broken and suffer from self-hatred and a myriad of other things. You will learn to utilize your armor and become their intercessor. This attack will not have power over you, and they will not win.

Ephesians 6:13-18 (NKJV)

¹³Therefore take up the whole armor of God, that you may be able to withstand in the evil day, and having done all, to stand. ¹⁴Stand therefore, having girded your waist with truth, having put on the breastplate of righteousness, ¹⁵and having shod your feet with the preparation of the gospel of peace; ¹⁶above all, taking the shield of faith with which you will be able to quench all the fiery darts of the wicked one. ¹⁷And take the helmet of salvation, and the sword of the Spirit, which is the word of God; [18]praying always with all prayer and supplication in the Spirit, being watchful to this end with all perseverance and supplication for all the saints.

You will discover that everyone who has done anything great has had to walk this same walk. Character and greatness come at a great price! People allow the enemy to use them to try to distract you, to discredit you, and yet you have the power to defeat him at every turn.

Personally, I have had to walk through several devastating lies and false accusations, learning that vengeance truly belongs to God and not to me. He will fight for me, if I can just keep my heart right and use my faith to destroy the unfruitful works of darkness.

What Is an Accusation?

An *accusation* is a statement by one person, asserting that another person or entity has done something improper. Accusations can be made with or without evidence; the accusation can be false, made out of malice, for the purpose of harming the reputation of the accused. The person who makes the accusation is an accuser, while the subject against whom it is made is the accused. A false accusation is a claim or allegation of wrongdoing that is untrue and/or otherwise unsupported by facts. False accusations are also known as groundless accusations, or unfounded accusations, or false allegations, or false claims. We will look at both true and false accusations throughout this book.

The Purpose of an Accusation

The purpose of an accusation is to charge someone with a crime. It is important to remember that an accusation comes about when someone thinks that another person has done something wrong. It doesn't mean, however, that the person is guilty.

Psychologists suggest that people's behavior can become irrational, causing them to operate out of character when falsely accused. If you are not believed, if you cannot fight back with the true story, or if now you are distrusted and under scrutiny, the sense of helplessness can be overwhelming.

***People in the Bible Who Suffered Accusations –
Some True and Some Untrue***

You will discover that you are in good company. The spirit of accusation started as far back as the Garden of Eden, when Satan accused God of trying to keep something from Adam and Eve.

***

> *"For God doth know that in the day ye eat thereof, then your eyes shall be opened, and ye shall be as gods, knowing good and evil" (Genesis 3:5 KJV).*

CHAPTER ONE

You Were Not Attacked; You Were Considered

Job's Accusation: Double for Your Trouble

As you have read in Revelation, there is an enemy who hates anyone who loves God and is referred to as *Satan*. You must understand that if the enemy targets you and accuses you before God, and if God allows it, then He knows you will pass the test. He has every confidence that even in pain, loss, and betrayal, you are a proven son or daughter. Let's look at the story of Job.

Job 1:1 (ERV)

There was a man named Job who lived in the country of Uz. He was a good, honest man. He respected God and refused to do evil.

Job 1:6-8 (KJV)

⁶Now there was a day when the sons of God came to present themselves before the LORD, and Satan came also among them. ⁷And the LORD said unto Satan, Whence comest thou? Then Satan answered the LORD, and said, From going to and fro in the earth, and from walking up and down in it. ⁸And the LORD saidunto Satan, Hast thou considered my servant Job, that there is none like him in the earth, a perfect and an upright man, one that feareth God, and escheweth evil?

As I read this text again, I was quickly reminded that God asked Satan the question, "Have you considered my servant Job?" There is no indication prior to this moment that the enemy was even focused on Job. It seems that Job was considered by God to be a man who would maintain his integrity even amid loss.

Once he had been targeted, he was accused of only serving God because of the possessions, the healing, and all the things that God had blessed him with. None of these things moved God, nor did the fact that Job was an upright man. When it is your time to be considered, you are being processed for the greatest move of God that you have ever experienced.

Job's situation did not look like a set-up for a blessing. It looked as if Job was being punished. As a matter of fact, his friends accused him of wrongdoing, suggesting that was why this had come upon him.

In a day he lost his children, his cattle, his home, and everything he possessed. There was always a messenger left that had witnessed the loss. I believe that God did that because He wanted someone to validate the events when the process was over. He had a wife who literally told him to curse God and die. What a helpmate! Can you even begin to imagine the heartbreak he must have felt? The disappointment that may have been overwhelming him? He had boils all over his body, he was homeless, and he was estranged from his wife, all while grieving the loss of his children.

Seemingly, when accusation hits your life, you are not facing that as your only giant. During the greatest accusation attack you may suffer from loss, grief, betrayal, and sickness, and it may seem as if life has hit you in every area imaginable. At that moment, you are at your wits' end and looking for a way out.

Have you ever been there, or perhaps you are there now? Maybe you have someone you love who has suffered multiple losses in a single day, and you are reading this book to find answers. Answers are truly what you look for when you are experiencing so much pain.

Job may have felt loss and felt let down by God, and may even have suffered greatly from depression. Isn't that what happens when we are in unexplainable circumstances? When there is no end to the pain? When you wake up every morning and go to bed every night looking for anything to break? Day after day, nothing changes. God is silent, and everyone around has something to say about why you are in the situation you are in.

We are not sure how long Job's trial lasted, but we know that it lasted months, according to the scriptures. No matter how long he suffered, it probably felt like an eternity. God allowed many people to see Job amid his suffering. When we are suffering, the worst thing that can happen is to have others watch.

Another thing that you will discover when a trial of this magnitude hits your life is how people respond to your situation and to you as an individual. Job's friends had to be rebuked by the Lord.

God wanted to show His goodness to Job to begin to repair the damage done to him. He had been allowed to go through all of this suffering because of a challenge from Satan, and the fact that God had him on display. As he received twice as much as he had before, I am sure that he had memories and had to battle the thoughts of losing his children. He received double for his trouble, but doubtless Job had much sadness and grief to overcome.

God did not undo Job's captivity until he prayed for his friends. So, you just may become your accuser's intercessor.

Job 42:10 (ERV)

Job prayed for his friends, and the LORD made Job successful again. The LORD gave him twice as much as he had before.

Paul Was Also Considered: Surviving the Snake Bite

Acts 28:5 (KJV)

And he shook off the beast into the fire, and felt no harm.

Paul had to endure remarkable pain to take the Gospel to the Gentiles. In 2 Corinthians 11:25, we read that he was shipwrecked three times. In Acts 27, we read that Paul was traveling on board a ship that ran into rocks and broke into pieces. In that moment of crisis, Paul became God's man on board the ship. He spoke the word of faith to the crew and passengers, and soon he oversaw the entire situation. Once he was in Melita, he worked with the other crew members to collect wood for a fire. A viper was hidden in the sticks he was carrying to lay on the fire. When he dropped the wood into the flames, the snake charged out of the pile of wood and bit Paul on the hand.

People Bites vs Snake Bites

Pause for a moment and put yourself in the place where Paul was, collecting the firewood. Now envision yourself reaching for a piece of wood, and there is a snke camouflaging itself to look like it was what you intended to gather. I want you to catch that. So many times, along our journey through life, we gather things unto ourselves because they look like what we need.

Our focus is somehow distorted, because things look like they will be valuable to what we are aiming to accomplish. The viper that bit Paul was believed to be a horned viper, or *Vipera ammodytes*, the formal term. This type of snake was known by the natives on the island of Melita to be very poisonous. In fact, it is known in the present day to be one of the most venomous vipers within Europe. They normally hide themselves in various places, sometimes camouflaging in open clearings, stockpiles, and rubble. These vipers generally only attack when provoked.

16

Believe it or not, there are spiritual snake bites that can come in the guise of human spirits. They are parallel to physical snake bites. When we come up against people "snake bites," that same venomous cycle begins. There are many things that would cause people to become provoked and strike against you. Let's use for an example a person such as a national voice coming against someone that no one knows. That would be considered as big, huge, and venomous to me.

These people have nothing to be compared to—national or international voices—in terms of notoriety, fame, or name recognition. However, for some reason the enemy has entered this individual and has caused this individual to take a bite out of another person's character, destiny, everything. One word from someone of this stature, just one word from somebody like that, having millions of followers, listeners, and supporters that hang on his every word, can have the deadliest and most devastating effects on your dreams, ministry, and even your businesses.

"People bites" can be the most confusing and the deadliest bites, especially when you have developed a close bond or relationship with them. Like horned vipers, they inconspicuously camouflage themselves. When you are unsuspecting, they lash out in an attempt to ultimately kill you. Oftentimes the church has the biggest instances of individuals administering those venomous "people bites," because of the low self-esteem suffered from low-level mindsets. Hurt people hurt people. They only way a person will attack any individual at all is if they feel empowered by taking away from who the person being attacked is, so that the accuser can be elevated and rise to the occasion.

Unfortunately, you even find this behavior in the actions of leaders. They have not been healed, and in some cases should not be leading people. Although this may be found to be true, we must understand that we all have flaws, and we must be willing to know that everyone is going through their own process.

Still, it is imperative that we remain in tune and focused during our daily life's journey. When we become distracted, our discernment is distorted and off. As the saying states so eloquently, we must "take the high road." We cannot stoop to our accuser's level. We must walk circumspectly in love, not holding on to senseless grudges like barbarians, regardless of what people do to us.

Now, place yourself on board the ship, like Paul. Can you imagine being shipwrecked? The experience in and of itself was an unbelievable one. The pieces from the boat and the roaring of the sea were enough to challenge anybody's faith. Yet he found a way to maintain his faith.

Have you found yourself in a situation where unimaginable things kept happening in your life, and it seemed as if God had just left you to the elements to die? The fear that emerged as the ship spiraled out of control and broke into pieces was enough to cause the greatest faith giant to waver.

Being accused of having been a murderer, on top of everything else, must have seemed like the final straw. All Paul wanted to do was to obey God. Oftentimes we forget that there is a cost to obeying God. Being considered by God in the midst of public display while being on trial causes you to draw attacks from people. Most of us in the church world know what it is to be attacked and kicked when we're down. This is a clear example of the warfare involved with your destiny.

Acts 28:3 (KJV) says, "And when Paul had gathered a bundle of sticks, and laid them on the fire, there came a viper out of the heat, and fastened on his hand." The Greek word *echidna* is the word used to describe a highly venomous snake. The Greek word *kathapto* means "tightly fastened." The viper not only bit the apostle Paul, it fastened on his arm very tightly. The viper released its full load of venom into his body.

The fire drew the viper out. Oftentimes, the fire of God that rests upon your life will draw out unusual attacks. Paul was considered the greatest apostle; he wrote more than two-thirds of the New Testament. Yet his life was filled with trials, accusations, and situations beyond most of our comprehension.

Acts 28:4 (KJV) says, "And when the barbarians saw the venomous beast hang on his hand, they said among themselves, No doubt this man is a murderer, whom, though he hath escaped the sea, yet vengeance suffereth not to live."

When the barbarians saw that Paul did not die, they assumed he was a god. How many times have people looked at you because of the last bite you took, expecting you to die? God will allow you to be bitten right in front of the ones accusing you and enable you to shake it off and walk out unharmed, before their very eyes. The mere fact that you were able to shake off what was supposed to have killed you is an indication of having a healthy spiritual immune system. A healthy spiritual immune system is when you don't feel the need to retaliate or prove to anyone that your accuser was wrong about you. Your immunity and tolerance levels in the supernatural are maintained by the intimate time of fellowship that you have with God in the glory realm or His secret place. Remember, you were not attacked, you were considered, so that God could use that death situation-that impossible feat-to reveal His glory. Paul was full of wisdom, so he used the opportunity to bring the entire island together for a crusade.

Publius, the chief of the island, was so impressed that he took Paul into his own home for three days. While Paul was with Publius, his father was sick with a fever and dysentery, and Paul went in and healed him.

Paul's greatest ministry was about to emerge. We know that God has called us, but we do not always recognize that the attacks that come up against us are to keep us from moving to the next level and dimension in God. Paul's life is proof perfect of this fact. The man was miraculously healed, and soon the entire island was in revival. This is what happens when great opposition comes against you, and accusation is a part of that process. By the time Paul departed Melita, he was so respected and honored that they loaded him down with everything necessary for the remainder of his journey!

We always believe that we know how we will respond in someone else's situation, until it is our own. Imagine being shipwrecked and losing all your belongings. After which, you wake up to find yourself marooned on an island inhabited by barbarians, and then a venomous viper bites you. In this instance, it is Paul who shakes it off, and revival breaks out. We have all thought of quitting at some point. I am sure Paul may have felt a bit discouraged even after seeing God turn disaster into revival. He still needed to heal from what he had been through. It did not vanish simply because God was using him mightily.

Many people move from disaster to revival without considering what they just went through, and how it has still affected them and has brought trauma into their lives. Healing is necessary after traumatic experiences, even during promotion.

Paul could have, however, used his trials as a reason to stop, slow down, or even go backwards. No matter the circumstance he faced, he kept pressing forward. God's power was available to give him victory in the midst of this season of trial. What is hindering you today? What is the devil trying to use to latch on to your life, to distract you? Why don't you make the decision to shake it off? There is more at stake than you can imagine. Many people are watching you through your ordeal, so you cannot lose focus. The enemy tries to get you to look at everything but God.

He (the enemy) wants you to live your life as if God has left you. He wants you to feel sorry for yourself and to wallow in self-pity. Truthfully, it is painful and tedious. You must find your victory in the Word of God. You must allow God to take what the enemy has meant for evil and turn it around, working it for your good. Make the devil sorry that he ever sent that poisonous viper to try to attack you by coming out stronger and more powerful in the Word.

God wants to prove to your enemies that what they were saying or may have heard concerning you was simply not true. You are not a sinner. You are not a barbarian. You are not the bottom of a barrel. You are not the things that they are accusing you of. Even if you have done what they are accusing you of, you're not who they say you are. When you carry greatness, everything and everybody around you is aware of it. The attacks and accusations may seem unbearable during the process, but if you continue to move forward, you will see double for all your trouble. God will reward you and give you a mighty testimony.

***

CHAPTER TWO

Plots and Plans

Joseph and His Family Set Up: Double for Your Trouble

Now think about the people you love. Have you ever loved someone who turned against you? Someone in your family, or a close friend—maybe even a spouse? The ultimate pain of betrayal comes when the accuser is someone that you love.

Personal Testimony

I remember the time when I was accused of something, and a family member called the authorities to investigate me. It was all fabricated. Nothing was true. I ran a private business with children, and the accusation that came was against me. I was accused of feeding the children spoiled food. When we were not looking, they crept into my business and unplugged my refrigerators and tried to get the food and formula to spoil. For some reason, that morning I felt led of the Lord to go in to work early and remodel the nursery.

I had no idea that this accusation was being brought against me. I completely remodeled the nursery and bought everything new, for no apparent reason. This was someone whom I had given a place to live and employment, so I had made a sacrifice to make sure that they were provided for, and they repaid me with an accusation.

Around two o'clock that day, we had a visitor requesting to see the area where I kept the children. To my surprise, it was a visit from the Department of Children and Families. The representative found that the place was immaculate, and none of the accusations were founded.

I was heartbroken and did not know how to process the fact that someone would try to ruin me and my business, simply out of purely evil intentions. It was a plot and a plan that the enemy had devised to try to bring destruction, but God intervened. I understand Joseph's plight when it comes to relatives.

Ultimately, Joseph was sold to Potiphar, the captain of Pharaoh's guard. Later, Joseph became Potiphar's personal servant, and subsequently his household's superintendent. Here, Potiphar's wife (called Zuleika in a later tradition) tried to seduce Joseph, which he refused. Angered by his running away from her, she made a false accusation of rape, and thus assured his imprisonment (Genesis 39:1-20).

In the biblical narrative, Joseph was sold into slavery by his jealous brothers and rose to become a vizier, the second most powerful man in Egypt next to Pharaoh, where his presence and office caused Israel to leave Canaan and settle in Egypt.

The story of Joseph is used to show that the journey to greatness is laced with testing, betrayal, processing, and trials. Joseph was a dreamer as a child, sharing his dreams with his family, who were not happy about what he shared as a dreamer. His brothers were jealous, and his father believed that he was filled with mischief. Unfortunately, his brothers devised a plan to get rid of him. After throwing him into a pit and dipping the coat of many colors that their father had given to Joseph in blood, they concocted a lie to tell their father that he had died. To further complete the deed, they sold him to a caravan of strangers. Can you imagine? Being a dreamer can be an extremely complicated thing when you are surrounded with people—even family—that refuse to deal with the jealousy in their hearts.

These brothers did not believe that Joseph deserved all that God had placed on his life. Many people do not feel that you deserve the blessings and open doors that God has given you. They will hate you for being blessed. They will lie about you and accuse you of the most terrible things. If you are not careful, your journey can cause you to believe that God Himself has forsaken you and turned you over to your persecutors.

Joseph is not admired as a dreamer:

"'Here comes that dreamer!' they said to each other" (Genesis 37:19 NIV).

A dreamer is one who dreams and has insight, and an inner knowing that there is more than that which can be seen with the natural eye. If you describe someone as a dreamer, you mean that they spend a lot of time thinking about and planning for things that they would like to happen, which seem improbable or impractical—yet they continue to believe. In essence, a dreamer is one who has insight and an inner knowing that there is more than what can be seen in the natural that must come to pass.

That is exactly the story of Joseph. In Genesis chapter 37, we see the life and journey of a young man who has been called "a dreamer" by his family. I genuinely believe that God allowed this story in the Word so that we can move forward in our dreams, and so we would understand that the life of the dreamer is laced with many unforeseen lessons.

Most of my life, I have been the one who steps out on faith, attempting to do many things. Others tend to think and say that it's easier for me, due to one reasoning or another. In reality, it has not been easy for me, and neither will it be easy for you. You must face the fact that uncommon producers endure uncommon attacks. You must outlive it, and you must do so without allowing what is happening to you to make you bitter or ashamed. Sometimes, God allows us to go through the most devastating seasons before we walk in the fullness of the things that He has for us. Let us look at the cost of *favor*.

Dreamers experience unsolicited *favor*

Genesis 37:4 (KJV)

And when his brethren saw that their father loved him more than all his brethren, they hated him, and could not speak peaceably unto him.

There is a saying that should be coined, and it is: "Favor ain't fair." It is not proper English or grammar, but it is a statement worth thinking about. When you are favored, many people are not happy for you or what you are about to walk into. In Genesis 37:4, Joseph's brothers could no longer speak peaceably to him because of the favor that rested on his life. In case you have been wondering why certain people will no longer speak to you, I would challenge to you ask the hard question: "Is it because of the favor that rests on my life?" These people are clearly letting you know that they are not the ones that should be connected to your life. If you allow them to stay, they will impede your progress. I know they may have been with you a long time, but if they are a dream killer, then you must choose to sever the tie, so that your dreams can live.

Jealousy is as cruel as the grave. Solomon mentions this in Song of Solomon 8:6. Joseph discovered this when his brothers plotted to kill him, simply because he had a dream that their father favored him most. Who are the people in your circle? You can clearly see that even your biological family can have issues with your favor and your dreams.

Dreamers are *hated*

Genesis 37:5 (KJV)

And Joseph dreamed a dream, and he told it to his brethren: and they hated him yet the more.

Hatred is a strong word, but it is how the scriptures define the emotion that Joseph's brothers felt toward him when he started to tell them his dream.

Be careful who you share your dreams with, and the way people respond when you do share them. They are giving you clues as to how they feel about you in their heart. They hated Joseph to the point to where they were plotting to kill him, but ended up selling him as a slave. It would appear that Joseph's dream was turning into a nightmare, and these are the stages we face when God starts to process us for the promise He has for us. He gives us the dream, and then He allows the stuff to happen to purge, purify, and perfect us.

Why am I sharing this with you? Simple—because you may be in the greatest battle of your life, and it looks like nothing is working; every door seems to be closed, all your friends have become haters, and ultimately it feels like God has left you. You have even experienced the ultimate betrayal of accusation that comes from your family. Cheer up! You are in good company. Anyone who has ever done anything great has a story. The story varies in content, but the structure is always the same. We all experience heartbreak, betrayal, lies, rejection, false accusations, misinterpretations of our motives, and pain. It is called "the process," and you *will* live through it. You will birth out the books, businesses, recordings, ministries, and everything else God has called you to bring forth. In many cases you need a coach that will not only help you push, but help you obtain your prize.

I know Joseph's story so well. I have lived it time and again, yet none of it was about to stop the plan that God had for my life. There are some delays, pitfalls, and setbacks woven into my story. Most of those came because of the choices I made and the people I allowed in my life.

Dreams are costly, and only an elect few will ever take the challenge and push until there is nothing left for them to do. My desire is, when I am finished here on the earth, that everything that was in my heart to do, I did it! I want to leave empty and make my contribution to the next generation. I want to leave a legacy.

Joseph is my favorite person to write about when it comes down to process, because he had multiple trials and an amazing outcome. There was one thing after another, yet you never really hear about the lingering effects of the accusations against him. The Word of God never states whether he was bitter, angry, or retaliatory, or if he spoke anything negative about Potiphar's wife. The only time we read about Joseph having any emotion is when he finally revealed to his brothers who he truly was when they were in the palace. It was at that time that there seems to have been a rush of reality, seen by Joseph, of what he had gone through.

Genesis 45:2 (KJV)

And he wept aloud: and the Egyptians and the house of Pharaoh heard.

I can relate to a lot of Joseph's story regarding process: losing things and being restored. I still cannot truly fathom that I went through what I went through. Joseph went through so much to have gotten to where he was, and it was almost as if none of it mattered (though he was grateful). There were times when I felt like Joseph, especially during the times of accusation and trial. Even when there were good times of blessings and doors opening that I was able to experience after all the devastating trials, the floodgate of what had happened began to fill my memories and to overwhelm all of the good things that were happening to me.

It was almost to the point where I didn't want to talk about the good things, because I still remembered the pain of the tragedies. Reflecting back, I remember going to a church service that I used to frequent, where the preacher prophesied over me that God was going to heal my memory. I didn't really think about my memory needing healing, but I am a living witness that until you allow God to heal the memory of your past, you'll never be able to fully embrace your now- not even your future. I had gotten so wrapped up and concerned, trying to figure it out—if nothing could stop it (the devastation) from happening to me before, what would stop or keep it from happening to me again? I analyzed everything under scrutiny. Would God actually do what He said? Did He really love me, like He said? You see, when you are traumatized, you begin making irrational decisions and entertaining thoughts that are contrary to the character of God.

I can imagine that with Joseph, there was a psychological warfare going on in his mind. Should we allow ourselves to feel the emotion and pain of what we experience through trials? Or should we become robot Christians who just quote scriptures and continue operating in life as if nothing ever happened, or that the sting of the pain didn't hurt? I shouted when I heard the infamous religious phrase "double for your trouble." I believed that I knew what that meant, but the older I got, the more I realized that I had compounding trauma which added to my feelings of being numb and distraught; I had never really released or peeled back the layers of my pain, and thus was never really able to manifest "double."

You may say to yourself, "Hey, that really doesn't affect me, because I've been through trouble before," but the trouble becomes heavier to carry when it's compounded. Like Joseph, this was trouble on another level, where I accusation. We all have our crosses to bear, but this was heavy and lonely. You may hear others say to you that we all have to walk alone at times, or we all have to die alone. The reality of those statements never really hits you until it's your time to travel down that path of loneliness. It's almost as if we deceive our own selves, hoping that we will never have to experience such painfulness or run into any setbacks.

The alone process is necessary, because it enables you to have a time of reset; if not, you wouldn't be able to properly discern the heart of the people around you. We repeat cycles of allowing "people biters" into our world when we don't take the time to see from clear angles. Remember, your job isn't to collect the red flags of "people biters," but to learn the lessons you need so that you won't repeat the toxic pattern and cycle of surrounding yourself with snake people, and to learn to dismiss them from your life.

There is so much more I could say about Joseph and his journey, and about me and my journey, but I will conclude with this: Genesis 50:20 (ERV), "It is true that you planned to do something bad to me. But really, God was planning good things. God's plan was to use me to save the lives of many people. And that is what happened."

So, my message to you today, dreamer, is to dream on. The process may be difficult and your heart may be broken, but just like Joseph, you are bigger than the place where you lived or those people you were around. There is a global anointing on you, which means you don't fit in with locals, regionals, or nationals—your dream is too big to fit, so He had to let them hate you so that you would not settle for good when you were pregnant with great.

***

CHAPTER THREE

Jealousy Is as Cruel as the Grave

Daniel's Accusation:
Divine Promotion

Song of Solomon 8:6 (KJV)

Set me as a seal upon thine heart, as a seal upon thine arm: for love is strong as death; jealousy is cruel as the grave: the coals thereof are coals of fire, which hath a most vehement flame.

Jealousy is a complex emotion that encompasses feelings ranging from fear of abandonment to rage to humiliation. It strikes people of all ages, genders, and sexual orientations, and is most typically aroused when a person perceives a threat to a valued relationship from a third party. The threat may be real or imagined. It is not limited to romantic relationships; jealousy can also arise among siblings competing for parental attention, among co-workers, or in friendships. Jealousy is distinguished from envy in that jealousy always involves a third party, seen as a rival for affection or attention. Envy occurs between only two people and is best summed up as, "I want what you have."

I remember being a victim of jealousy. I received an email from a person who literally wrote how they were jealous of my life. Now, most people will not admit when they are jealous, but this person was extremely bold about it. In the story of Daniel, we see that there were individuals surrounding Daniel who didn't like the fact that he lived uprightly, was committed to praying, and remained faithful to the God that he served. Ironically, it always seems that those who have more than you are the main ones who are jealous of you.

Whenever someone makes it blatantly known that they are jealous of you, you want to stand guard. For the next several years, I found myself being confronted and warring with someone who practiced and had witchcraft tendencies. I had a business relationship with this individual, which made it uncomfortable to know that they were not for me. I thought that the individual's impression of me would pass if I gave them an opportunity, but in the end it turned out to be most detrimental. It got to the point where they had another individual contact me who was a witch, wanting me to join them. Yes, they actually wanted to recruit me to be like them!

The enemy can be bold in his tactics to completely destroy you, naturally and spiritually. The individual who was jealous of me recognized my spiritual giftings and tried to entice me to pervert my giftings. If the enemy can't get you one way, he'll try to slither himself into another. Sadly, these individuals love to have positions of prominence so that they can manipulate and then strike down to destroy! Jealousy is as cruel as the grave, because people will try to kill you, so that you don't survive.

Daniel 6:1-5 (NKJV)

[1]It pleased Darius to set over the kingdom one hundred and twenty satraps, to be over the whole kingdom; [2]and over these, three governors, of whom Daniel was one, that the satraps might give account to them, so that the king would suffer no loss. [3]Then this Daniel distinguished himself above the governors and satraps, because an excellent spirit was in him; and the king gave thought to setting him over the whole realm. [4]So the governors and satraps sought to find some charge against Daniel concerning the kingdom; but they could find no charge or fault, because he was faithful; nor was there any error or fault found in him. [5]Then these men said, "We shall not find any charge against this Daniel unless we find it against him concerning the law of his God."

When you are faced with the riveting clinch of someone else's insecurities, be careful and mindful of that individual. That is what was happening to Daniel—he had become a target. The king was pleased to set Daniel over the whole kingdom. He had an excellent spirit, which meant he had a character that could be trusted even when no one was looking. He was so committed to walking uprightly that his accusers could not find a single accusation against him, so they attacked his love for God.

Was the reason for your attack because you chose to love God and walk uprightly? There are many times when we are attacked because we refuse to back down from our stand to live for God and to pray. There are intimidating voices roaring around you, trying to cause your demise, simply because you have an excellent spirit.

When we are attacked for seemingly no reason, we sometimes begin to look at our own lives as though we have done something wrong. We find ourselves saying within, and telling others, "But I did nothing wrong"; soon afterwards, you realize that you are under attack.

When this happens to you, do not feel the need to talk about your accuser or the accusation. Stay focused on what you are determined to do as it relates to your relationship with God. You cannot change who you are because people do not like you. You cannot follow the wide path when you are destined for the narrow one. You cannot compromise, nor can you be moved by the persecution.

Daniel 6:6-10 (NKJV)

⁶So these governors and satraps thronged before the king, and said thus to him: "King Darius, live forever! ⁷All the governors of the kingdom, the administrators and satraps, the counselors and advisors, have consulted together to establish a royal statute and to make a firm decree, that whoever petitions any god or man for thirty days, except you, O king, shall be cast into the den of lions. ⁸Now, O king, establish the decree and sign the writing, so that it cannot be changed, according to the law of the Medes and Persians, which does not alter." ⁹Therefore King Darius signed the written decree. ¹⁰Now when Daniel knew that the writing was signed, he went home. And in his upper room, with his windows open toward Jerusalem, he knelt down on his knees three times that day, and prayed and gave thanks before his God, as was his custom since early days.

Daniel had always prayed since his early days. He could not change who he was just because they had enticed the king to make a decree. Sometimes when you are excelling, others become jealous because they feel they should hold the position that you have been granted.

They (the accusers) were not men of integrity or with an excellent spirit. They did not qualify for the same position that Daniel was appointed to. People want promotion when they do not deserve it, and they do not want you to have it. Daniel was also being tested by God to see what he'd do when plotted and planned against. Would you have remained faithful to prayer? Would you have tried to defend yourself? Daniel was not moved by the decree, and after he found out about it, he went home, knelt, and prayed three times that day, giving thanks before his God.

Daniel 6:11-17 (NKJV)

¹¹Then these men assembled and found Daniel praying and making supplication before his God. ¹²And they went before the king, and spoke concerning the king's decree: "Have you not signed a decree that every man who petitions any god or man within thirty days, except you, O king, shall be cast into the den of lions?" The king answered and said, "The thing is true, according to the law of the Medes and Persians, which does not alter." ¹³So they answered and said before the king, "That Daniel, who is one of the captives from Judah, does not show due regard for you, O king, or for the decree that you have signed, but makes his petition three times a day." ¹⁴And the king, when he heard these words, was greatly displeased with himself, and set his heart on Daniel to deliver him; and he labored till the going down of the sun to deliver him. ¹⁵Then these men approached the king, and said to the king, "Know, O king, that it is the law of the Medes and Persians that no decree or statute which the king establishes may be changed." ¹⁶So the king gave the command, and they brought Daniel and cast him into the den of lions. But the king spoke, saying to Daniel, "Your God, whom you serve continually, He will deliver you." ¹⁷Then a stone was brought and laid on the mouth of the den, and the king sealed it with his own signet ring and with the signets of his lords, that the purpose concerning Daniel might not be changed.

Have you ever been in a situation where you were clearly persecuted or accused just for following God or His Word? That is what Daniel was facing. He had been accused of violating the king's decree, having been set up by those who did not qualify for his position. Isn't it amazing that people want what you have, but they are not willing to pay the same price that you pay? The interesting thing is that Daniel was not moved by fear, by threats, or by intimidating forces. He decided that he would rather continue to be faithful to his time with God than to succumb to the king's decree. When you have a prayer life with God, He will remove the fear of man. It was his time of prayer that went ahead of him to the lion's den. The time of prayer with God had made divine provision for Daniel. He prayed until there was divine assistance.

Daniel Saved from the Lions

Daniel 6:18-22 (NKJV)

¹⁸Now the king went to his palace and spent the night fasting; and no musicians were brought before him. Also his sleep went from him. ¹⁹Then the king arose very early in the morning and went in haste to the den of lions. ²⁰And when he came to the den, he cried out with a lamenting voice to Daniel. The king spoke, saying to Daniel, "Daniel, servant of the living God, has your God, whom you serve continually, been able to deliver you from the lions?" ²¹Then Daniel said to the king, "O king, live forever! ²²My God sent His angel and shut the lions' mouths, so that they have not hurt me, because I was found innocent before Him; and also, O king, I have done no wrong before you."

God *is* the God of vengeance, and I don't believe that anybody can get away with anything when He is in the midst. As you see in this text of scripture, there was divine, supernatural intervention into the affairs of Daniel's life. He was untouchable in the face of angry, hungry lions, because prayer had prevailed and moved the divine into the den before he ever got there. God sent an angel and shut the lions' mouths. Do not worry about the threats of the enemy when you are innocent. There is no need to try to convince people that the lies are coming from the enemy. You only need to pray, believe, and refuse to back down. It is all a plot from the enemy to affect your time with God. Do you make way for petty distractions?

Daniel 6:23 (NKJV)

²³Now the king was exceedingly glad for him, and commanded that they should take Daniel up out of the den. So Daniel was taken up out of the den, and no injury whatever was found on him, because he believed in his God.

God took what the enemy meant for evil and worked it for Daniel's good. As you see in the text, what was meant for evil towards Daniel, God turned around for his good. The very sentence that was set for Daniel was now set for his accusers. A lot of times, we will read these as if they are kids' stories. I can assure you, this is *not* a cute story. Even Simba is scary when he begins to roar. Anyone who sees a lion understands that it is a ferocious animal, and that it is not a game. It is a matter of surviving the threat to be eaten and killed. This is much worse than a people or snake bite, because you can be ripped to shreds.

The triumph of this text is that he stood, and now he was walking in more supernatural favor than before, and God used it as a witness, resulting in the king believing in Daniel's God. Your story is not as bad as the enemy tries to make you to believe. God will use every negative situation in your life to bring people to the saving power of God. Not only that, your trial brings with it a divine promotion.

King Darius Honors God

Daniel 6:24-28 (NKJV)

24 And the king gave the command, and they brought those men who had accused Daniel, and they cast them into the den of lions-them, their children, and their wives; and the lions overpowered them, and broke all their bones in pieces before they ever came to the bottom of the den. 25 Then King Darius wrote: To all peoples, nations, and languages that dwell in all the earth: Peace be multiplied to you. 26 I make a decree that in every dominion of my kingdom men must tremble and fear before the God of Daniel. For He is the living God, and steadfast forever; His kingdom is the one which shall not be destroyed, and His dominion shall endure to the end. 27 He delivers and rescues, and He works signs and wonders in heaven and on earth, who has delivered Daniel from the power of the lions. 28 So this Daniel prospered in the reign of Darius and in the reign of Cyrus the Persian.

God Is the God of Vengeance

Romans 12:19 (KJV)

Dearly beloved, avenge not yourselves, but rather give place unto wrath: for it is written, Vengeance is mine; I will repay, saith the Lord.

You and I are not permitted to operate in revenge, but you can call on the Lord of vengeance. *Revenge* means the action of inflicting hurt or harm on someone for an injury or wrong suffered at their hands. *Vengeance* means punishment inflicted or retribution exacted for an injury or wrong. God executes vengeance because He is just and knows all things, but when we take matters into our own hands, we open ourselves up to the enemy taking advantage of us. Trust God and His way of doing things. The more you decide to be quiet and let the Lord fight your battles, the better off you will be. You can clearly see this in the life of Daniel and his love for his God.

Psalm 109:4 (NASB)

In return for my love they act as my accusers; but I am in prayer.

***

CHAPTER FOUR

Pray for Vengeance, Not Revenge

David's Accusation:
Winning in Adversity, Lies, and Plots

Romans 12:19 (CSB)

Friends, do not avenge yourselves; instead, leave room for God's wrath, because it is written, Vengeance belongs to me; I will repay, says the Lord.

God is able to handle those who hate you for no reason, those who will try to destroy you, and those who will try to set traps for you. You must understand: it is not your job to repay people for the evil that they do to you. A Christian who tries to take revenge is presumptuous. He claims for himself a role that belongs to God.

Revenge is both a noun and a verb, and generally means " the act of taking vengeance for injuries or wrongs, retaliation." While *revenge* can function as a verb, it is much more common for it to be a noun. *Revenge* is a more personal form of vengeance and is usually centered around feelings of anger and resentment.

The Bible refers to divine retribution as, in most cases, being delayed or "treasured up" for a future time. Some religions or philosophical positions have no concept of divine retribution, nor posit a God being capable of or willing to express such human sentiments as jealousy, vengeance, or wrath.

God will bring vengeance, retribution, and recompense to your life for every time you have to stand and endure these types of accusations. Regardless of what people believe, God is a god of vengeance! He will fight for you.

This brings us to why David the psalmist would write such a psalm. Psalm 109 reflects a common problem which we have all experienced. The psalm describes the reactions of a man who has been unjustly accused, wrongly treated. He has been set upon by those who are attempting to destroy him, yet without a cause. The psalm also is a problem psalm. One need only read it to be troubled about this psalm. Why should this strange, extravagant language of hostility against another human being be included in the Book of Psalms?

We shall attempt an answer to that as we go through the exposition of this psalm. Have you ever had to endure such unjust accusations, to the point that you would want to pray or write such a psalm as this?

Notice that it is a psalm of David, and therefore reflects an experience which David went through. It is difficult to tell exactly which of his recorded experiences is referred to. When we are faced with such adversity, many times people misunderstand our plight. David shows us what it really looks like when you are in the middle of a process.

Each of us has a process to greatness, and we all will face accusation. God spoke to me during the greatest lies ever told about me, saying that many who have gone where I am going have already gone through what I was going through. Tears ran down my face in total shock at how the enemy can erect schemes and plans against our lives, and how people allow him to use them against us. There is no pain like that of betrayal coupled with lies.

As we explore this psalm, I want you to imagine and heal from the past lies and accusations that you have had to live through. Pray to the Lord of vengeance, and watch Him deliver you from the snares of the enemy.

The opening words of the psalm set before us the problem this man faces:

Psalm 109:1-5 (RSV)

¹Be not silent, O God of my praise!
²For wicked and deceitful mouths are opened against me,
speaking against me with lying tongues.
³They beset me with words of hate, and attack me without cause.
⁴In return for my love they accuse me, even as I make prayer for them.
⁵So they reward me evil for good, and hatred for my love.

Here is a man who is under attack from rather unscrupulous persons. Those who attack him so bitterly are obviously not to be trusted. "They are deceitful," he says, "they are wicked," i.e., they are determined upon evil, and they are thoroughly unscrupulous; they do not care what they say or what they do. With lying tongues, they are out to destroy.

When I was married, I remember not really knowing what I brought to the table. There were gifts and talents lying dormant on the inside of me that I wasn't aware of. It wasn't until my thirties that I finally learned how to type or use a computer, for that matter. Then, I discovered my gift of speaking and administration. I also grew to become a good worshipper in song, and I loved who I was becoming. As the gifts began to grow and become polished, a wedge began to grow in my marriage. While advancing in ministry together, the same person who I thought would cover my weaknesses began to display and expose them publicly. That began tearing away at my confidence level, and I began struggling between being who God had called me to be and who someone else wanted me to remain. Doubt began to flood the back of my mind whenever someone else said anything good about me. Your covering is everything. Spiritually, I was ahead of my time. I was the one who stepped out in faith and took chances.

I never imagined that I would have to withstand so much ridicule—not just on the outside, but on the inside of my home. Like David, I had to decide to wear my own armor, and not something that didn't belong to me. I embraced who God called me to be, even in the midst of things that seemed like giants, taunting me.

Perhaps some of you have had this experience. You have been unjustly accused by someone who has deliberately sought to slander you, to besmirch your character, or to ruin your reputation, and you know just how this David felt. Furthermore, these people in this particular psalm are wholly unjustified in this attack. He says they do this "without a cause," at least as far as the psalmist can see, and we take him to be an honest man. He sees absolutely no reason for their accusations. They are afflicting him, upsetting him, and attacking him without him having given them any reason to do so.

In verses 4-5 it is apparent that this man has tried to remedy the situation, but it has come to a place where it is humanly hopeless. He has tried to answer these people in the right way. He says,

Psalm 109:4-5 (RSV)

⁴In return for my love they accuse me, even as I make prayer for them. ⁵So they reward me evil for my good, and hatred for my love.

This man understands that "a soft answer turns away wrath" (Proverbs 15:1 RSV), and he has tried that with them. He has followed the New Testament standard of praying for those who hate him and despitefully use him. It is remarkable, is it not, that here in the Old Testament you find such a clear demonstration of the fulfillment of the New Testament requirement to pray for our enemies? We are to love those who persecute us and try to do good toward them. This man has done that, yet it has not altered the situation. His enemies have not ceased their attack; they are just as vicious, just as malicious, just as fiercely hostile as they were before, and now he does not know what to do next. This is the problem that faces him at this point.

Can you imagine doing your part in loving people and doing what you know is right, yet they will not stop? I know exactly what he is experiencing. I had a lie erected against me, and it was so painful and damaging to me. It was a huge, public lie, set forth by the enemy to destroy my influence as a minister and as a person. The person decided to take it public on social media—actually, it happened through three different people at three different times.

My natural instinct is to fight back. It is the way I have lived most of my life: fighting back. However, it was a different season of my life, and I was required to be silent. I had to take the lies and accusations. I could not present my side of the story in any one of the situations. I had to let them believe the lies. I had to learn how to outlive the lies. You may ask: did I pray Psalm 109? ...I decline to answer!

Now according to the next verses, it sounds as though he gives up. He has tried the right thing, and it does not work, so he gives up. It is very much as you sometimes hear the Sermon on the Mount quoted. "If someone slaps you on the right cheek, turn to him the other cheek" (Matthew 5:39 NCV)—and then, *pow*, let him have it! It almost sounds as though this man is doing this. He has tried the right thing, and when it doesn't work, he lets them have it. Listen to the cruel and bitter words that pour out!

Psalm 109:6-15 (RSV)

⁶Appoint a wicked man against him; let an accuser bring him to trial. [Literally it is, "stand at his right hand" and means to accuse him in court.] ⁷When he is tried, let him come forth guilty; let his prayer be counted as sin!

⁸May his days be few; may another seize his goods! 9May his children be

43

fatherless, and his wife a widow! *¹⁰May his children wander about and beg; may they be driven out of the ruins they inhabit!*

¹¹May the creditor seize all that he has; may strangers plunder the fruits of his toil! *¹²Let there be none to extend kindness to him, nor any to pity his fatherless children!* *¹³May his posterity be cut off; may his name be blotted out in the second generation!*

¹⁴May the iniquity of his fathers be remembered before the Lord, and let not the sin of his mother be blotted out! *¹⁵Let them be before the lord continually; and may his memory be cut off from the earth!*

What strong language! What hostility! How fierce is the harshness here! Some of you are trying to memorize this so you will remember to say it the next time a suitable occasion arises! This passage has raised the problem of so- called "imprecatory psalms," these psalms which seem to heap imprecations, maledictions, against people. Many have been troubled by these, and this is the worst of them all. There is no stronger language in the psalms. We have chosen the toughest one of all to deal with. There were several times when I felt the desire to pray this prayer over my enemies.

How do you explain language like this in the psalms? What do you do with this? Well, it seems to me that the clearest and simplest answer is that this is not one of the imprecatory psalms at all. This man is not saying this himself but is quoting what his enemies say about him. In Hebrew, there is no way of indicating a quotation as we do in English, with quotation marks. There are no quotation marks in Hebrew, so the psalmist simply must run on. But there are several things which give us a clue here:

Firstly, you will notice a very remarkable and immediate change of attitude between verses 5 and 6. In verse 5 he says, "They reward me evil for good" (i.e., I am doing good to them; they do evil back), "and hatred for my love." Now it seems to me incredible that a man should so suddenly turn from an expression of love and of warmth to one of such violent and appalling invective. So, there is a drastic change of attitude which comes in here.

Secondly, there is a change of number that occurs. We must have a little lesson in grammar here. Notice that in verses 1-5 you have his enemies referred to in the plural: "them," "they"; but now suddenly it has become "he." If this psalmist is going on now describing what he wants to have happen to his enemies, it is difficult to explain this sudden change of number. Why does it suddenly become "he" instead of "they"? But if what he is doing is quoting what they say about him, it makes perfect sense. The harsh words fit best in the mouths of the psalmist's accusers.

This is confirmed by the fact that in the Jewish version of the Old Testament, verse 20, which is the conclusion of this quoted portion, instead of reading, "May this be the reward of my accusers from the Lord," says instead, "This is the reward which my accusers seek from the Lord, those who speak evil against my life!"

This would confirm, therefore, that this entire portion, from verse 6 through verse 19, should be put in quotation marks. Perhaps you might like to mark your own Bible that way. He is simply revealing what these people have said about him that distresses him so and which makes him cry out before God. They are so fierce and unrelenting in their hostility, and from their language, we get a glimpse of the intensity of their hatred.

Even though he probably wanted to utter these words against his accusers, it is not him speaking about his desire, but the things they are speaking against him. The sting of lies, hatred, and evil seem to plague us as we attempt to find our purpose and destiny. It is because the enemy uses accusations as a final attempt to gain our attention and focus. Do not give in or allow this to happen; sure, it hurts, and I am sure you may have sleepless nights, but allow God to develop your character amid this adversity. Choose the Word of God over your fleshly desire for revenge.

In verses 6-15 there is a revelation of the strategy they have devised against him. Notice what they are after. First, they want to rig a false trial. They want to get him before the law on a false charge and arrange a false witness to accuse him, and thus gain a legal condemnation. Note thecleverness of these people. They are not going to waylay him and murder him; they would be open to charges themselves if they did that, but they are going to destroy him legally. They have figured out a way by which they can rig the trial and get him condemned, and do it all legally. Then they mean to accomplish his death. They want a death sentence.

If you have had liars and accusations pierce you from within, you know the level of pain the psalmist is experiencing. They don't want him dead; they just want to destroy him. If you are prophetic in any way, there is a remnant out there that hates you enough to do such evil against you. Your prayer life and your prayer covering are vital when this type of attack has been launched against you.

Psalm 109:8-10 (RSV)

[8]*May his days be few...*
[9]*May his children be fatherless, and his wife a widow!*
[10]*May his children wander about and beg.*

Clearly, they are out to destroy him physically. Then they want to take everything he has. Their hatred is so terrible that they want to leave nothing for his wife and children, but wish to destroy them as well.

Psalm 109:11-12 (RSV)

[11]May the creditor seize all that he has...
[12]Let there be none to extend kindness to him, nor any to pity his fatherless children!

Finally, so fierce, so appalling is their revenge that they even want to carry it on before God himself. The attempt is made on their part to seek his eternal damnation. Their prayer is,

Psalm 109:13-15 (RSV)

[13]May his posterity be cut off; may his name be blotted out in the second generation! [14]May the iniquity of his fathers be remembered before the Lord... [15]Let them be before the Lord continually; and may his memory be cut off from the earth!

To put it bluntly, what they are asking for is that God should damn this man. They are saying, "God, destroy him!" Now is it not rather revealing that this is the most common oath heard today? When hatred rises in the heart, the easiest thing for men to say is, "God, destroy him!" Hatred seeks the ultimate destruction, even the eternal destruction of an individual. The ultimate wish of hate is that God would bring the man to damnation.

Now the psalmist lists the reasons his enemies give for this vituperation. What is it that this man has done that makes them so vindictive, so filled with fierce hatred? He lists the two reasons they set forth. First,

Psalm 109:16 (RSV)

For he did not remember to show kindness,
but pursued the poor and needy
and the brokenhearted to their death.

From their point of view, that was the way it looked. You can see in this that strange twisting of reason that occurs when we act in self-defense; that strange rationalizing by which we appear to be ourselves the victims of injustice, even though we may well deserve what is happening to us. This is what these men are feeling. They are blaming this poor man, saying that he did not remember to show kindness but pursued the poor and needy and brokenhearted to their death—but all the time it was they who were doing it.

I would like to think that none of you have ever had to live through such an attack. However, I am sure you are reading this book because you are trying to understand why this attack is coming against you. There is no reason other than the fact that you refuse to quit. Your perseverance is intimidating, and they do not like your favor. This is happening to a man whose destiny is great, yet the spirit of attack is no respecter of persons. The process is costly! The manifestation is even more costly, but you can do this.

Even when David was the only valiant warrior who stood up against the giant Goliath, he refused to back down or use any armor that didn't belong to him. God blessed him with the ingenuity, skill, and wisdom to use a slingshot and five smooth stones to defeat the very thing that seemed greater than everyone who was watching him thought he was. That speaks volumes, because a lot of times we may not have what everyone else is bringing to the table, but we're fearless. As the story of David progresses, we see how the view of how he is seen shifts and morphs into that of a hero, but you still have those who desire him to fail. We see how Saul does everything he can to take his life, so David is on the run.

It is amazing to me how many people will try to sabotage your greatness, but I recognize that this is their assignment from the evil one. They become committed to the cause of your demise and destruction. You win! That is the conclusion of the matter—*you win!*

The second reason for his enemies' hatred is like the first. They said of him,

Psalm 109:17-18a (RSV)

> ¹⁷*He loved to curse; let curses come on him!*
> *He did not like blessing; may it be far from him!*
> ¹⁸*He clothed himself with cursing as his coat.*

Again, they are blaming him to justify their own cursing. They have just cursed him; they have just said, "May God destroy you!" But to justify it, they say, "Well, that's what he said to us!" Again, this is human nature, is it not?

I remember fighting as a child, and if someone asked, "Who started this?" my response would always be that it was because of what the other person did to me. How true that is to our nature. We love to blame the other. We accuse others of the very things for which we are guilty. That is what is happening here. Notice how they intensify this.

Psalm 109:18b-19 (RSV)

¹⁸*...may it [these curses] soak into his body like water, like oil into his bones!* ¹⁹*May it be like a garment which he wraps round him, like a belt with which he daily girds himself!*

So terrible is their hatred, so malevolent is their fierce reaction, that they intensify their language to the ultimate refinement of malice. They pour out invective upon him to justify their own hate. Before we go on to look at the psalmist's reaction, perhaps it might be well to note one further thing in this section. In verse 8 are words which are taken by the Holy Spirit and applied, in the New Testament, to Judas Iscariot.

Psalm 109:8 (RSV)

May his days be few; may another seize his goods!

Or literally, "May another take his office!" You will recall that in the first chapter of Acts, the eleven apostles are gathered to appoint a successor to Judas. Peter quotes from two of the psalms to justify that appointment. One of them is Psalm 69:25 (KJV), which states, "Let their habitation be desolate," and the other is this verse from Psalm 109:8 (KJV), "Let another take his office." This has raised the suggestion that perhaps this whole passage applied to Judas—that it is all a prediction of the terrible fate that would await Judas Iscariot: his wife and children would be left desolate, and he himself would be destroyed by God.

Now let us look at the reaction of this man. Here he is, in this terrible situation, with his enemies attempting to take his life. He has tried the right way to react, but it does not seem to work. He does not know what to do now. He cries before God, in the literal rendering of verse 20,

Psalm 109:20 (Literal)

This is the reward which my accusers seek from the Lord, those who speak evil against my life!

What shall he do? Well, what he does is beautiful. He commits the whole matter to the Lord in prayer. This closing prayer of the psalm is a marvelous picture of the right attitude, the right reaction, the right way to handle this kind of a situation. Listen to it.

Psalm 109:21-25 (RSV)

[21]But thou, O God my Lord, deal on my behalf for thy name's sake; because thy steadfast love is good, deliver me! [22]For I am poor and

needy, and my heart is stricken within me. ²³I am gone, like a shadow at evening; I am shaken off like a locust. ²⁴My knees are weak through fasting; my body has become gaunt. ²⁵I am an object of scorn to my accusers; when they see me, they wag their heads.

Notice that the first thing he does is to commit the cause to God. "Thou, O God of my life, deal on my behalf for thy name's sake!" Here is a man who understands the nature of reality. He understands how life operates. He understands the truth behind the admonition of scripture, both in the Old and New Testament: "Vengeance is mine, says the Lord; I will repay" (Deuteronomy 32:35, Romans 12:19). Vengeance is mine! Don't you try it; don't you attempt it! Don't try to "get even," because if you do, you'll only make the matter worse. You will perpetuate a feud that may go on for years—even for centuries—destroying, wrecking, and damaging others and creating all kinds of difficulties, both for them and for you. No, no—vengeance is mine, says the Lord. I am the only one who has the wisdom adequate to handle this kind of a problem. This man recognizes that and commits the cause to God.

But he also understands something else. He understands that God's name is involved in all of this. When God's people are being persecuted, then God is also being persecuted. His name is involved in it. It is up to God to defend that name, not man. Recall that when Saul of Tarsus was converted on the Damascus road, and the Lord Jesus appeared to him in a light brighter than the sun, Saul cried out to him and said, "Lord, who are you?" Jesus said, "I am Jesus, whom you are persecuting." Saul was persecuting the Christians, but when he was persecuting them, he was also persecuting the Lord. God is involved in His people's trials.

God is involved in what happens to His own. The psalmist, understanding this, commits the whole cause to God and says, "God, you deal with it. It is your problem. Your name is involved; you handle it on my behalf for your name's sake." Is that not a thoroughly Christian reaction? Listen to Peter, as he shows us that this was exactly the reaction of the Lord Jesus Himself.

So, when they do it to you, they are also doing it to Him. He loves you with an everlasting love, and He will personally handle those who conspire against you. Just hold on and keep the faith. Stand firmly on the Word of God. Continue to build your faith and confidence in God, and watch how masterfully He will reconcile your life and bring you great reward. Jesus was innocent, and yet he was accused; should you expect anything less?

1 Peter 2:22-23 (RSV)

[22]He committed no sin; no guile was found on his lips. [23]When he was reviled, he did not revile in return; when he suffered, he did not threaten; but he trusted to him who judges justly.

Peter says that He has left us an example, that we should follow in His steps. He trusted Himself to Him who judges justly. Dr. F. B. Meyer has said, "We make a mistake in trying always to clear ourselves. We should be wiser to go straight on, humbly doing the next thing, and leaving God to vindicate us." There may come hours in our lives when we shall be misunderstood, slandered, falsely accused. Fret not: "He shall bring forth thy righteousness as the light, and thy judgment as the noonday" (Psalm 37:6 KJV). At such times it is exceedingly difficult not to act on the policy of the men around us in the world. They at once appeal to law and force and public opinion. But the believer takes his case into a higher court and lays it before his God.

That is what this man has done. He has laid it before God. Then he cries out for strength. He himself is in need.

Psalm 109:22-24 (RSV)

²²For I am poor and needy, and my heart is stricken within me. ²³I am gone, like a shadow at evening; I am shaken off like a locust. ²⁴My knees are weak through fasting; my body has become gaunt.

It is a difficult thing to endure slander. It is hard; it does something to you; it takes something out of you. Have you ever falsely accused someone and never gone back to make it right? Put yourself in the place of the accuser and look at your situation through those eyes.

The psalmist asks for vindication, and he does it on two grounds.

Psalm 109:26-28a (RSV)

²⁶Help me, O Lord my God!
Save me according to thy steadfast love!
²⁷Let them know that this is thy hand; thou,
O Lord, hast done it!
²⁸Let them curse, but do thou bless!

You can pray this prayer concerning your situation.

Psalm 109:28b-29 (Indicative Mood)

²⁸My assailants shall be put to shame, and thy servant shall be glad!
²⁹My accusers shall be clothed with dishonor;
they shall be wrapped in their own shame as in a mantle!

Now notice what this man is doing. He is asking God to vindicate him, but to do it in such a way as to reveal the fact that God is doing it. He says, "Now, Lord, let them curse. I can't stop them, and You may not choose to, but if You let them curse, bless me anyhow so that they will see that You are not cursing me; it is they who are doing it. Give me inner strength, inner blessing, so that I can remain calm, untroubled, and un-distressed during the cursing. Then men will see that it is Your hand that is holding me up, Your hand that is strengthening me. Second, do it in such a way as to make the accusers ashamed of themselves." Now he does not mean "put to shame" in the sense of heaping scorn and humiliation upon them; he means let them be ashamed of themselves—let them see the facts in such a light that eventually they'll be sorry, be ashamed that they ever attempted anything like this, because it is so unjustified. "Lord, vindicate me in that way."

Once again this is exactly in line with the New Testament. Again, in 1 Peter, chapter 3, Peter says,

1 Peter 3:16 (RSV)

And [you who are abused] keep your conscience clear, so that, when you are abused, those who revile your good behavior in Christ may be put to shame.

Do not allow people to draw you into their drama. It is their issue and not yours. Refuse to participate. Do not allow them to change who you are and destroy the word God has used to refine your character. When they strike, refuse to strike back; refuse to attack or get even; never avenge yourself—just let it happen and watch God.

Thank God for every opportunity to let His love shine through you. You will be criticized, attacked, suffer persecution and affliction, but do not allow impurity to destroy your good testimony. Learn to walk through the fire and refuse to be burned. Choose love. You can achieve this goal, but you must surrender to God.

The goal of the enemy is to get you to abort your own destiny. He can't do it, so he will try to use your words or find an open door to accuse you before God. This is the note on which this psalm closes. It is a note of ringing affirmation, of confidence.

Psalm 109:30-31 (RSV)

³⁰With my mouth I will give great thanks to the Lord; I will praise him in the midst of the throng. ³¹For he stands at the right hand of the needy, to save him from those who condemn him to death.

Recall that, in verse 6, this man's enemies had wanted to appoint an accuser to stand at his right hand and condemn him. But he closes the psalm by saying that he realizes it is God who stands at the right hand of the needy, God who makes their cause His own, God who knows a thousand ways to work it all out—without violence, without the perpetuation of hatred, without the destruction of lives—to bring truth to light and to establish the facts in such a way that even the accusers will be ashamed of themselves

that they ever attempted such a thing. How wise it is to commit our cause to God in times like this.

What I like about David is that after he's finished having javelins thrown at him, he enters into the second phase of his process. He now enters a cave with 400 men who are in debt, distressed, and discouraged. There David is, with these overlooked men whom nobody else sees the potential in, and he turns them into valiant men. He's preparing his team that will travel with him as he journeys on to the palace to become king. So, David went from the cave to the kingdom, with a dream team that would help propel his destiny. Not only were the men valiant and heavily gifted with talents, but they were *all* prosperous and able to give unto the kingdom great wealth.

Choose to take a praise break by thanking God for all the things you have been able to survive, and the fact that this thing has made you a better person.

***

CHAPTER FIVE

*Jesus and the Woman
Caught in Adultery:*

*When You Are Guilty
of the Accusation*

Jesus and the woman caught in adultery is found in John 7:53-8:11. In the passage, Jesus is sitting down in the temple to teach some of the people after He spent time at the Mount of Olives. A group of scribes and Pharisees confronts Jesus, interrupting His teaching session. They bring a woman, accusing her of committing adultery, claiming she was caught in the very act. They ask Jesus whether the punishment for someone like her should be stoning, as prescribed by the Mosaic Law.

Jesus first ignores the interruption and writes on the ground, as though He does not hear them. But when the woman's accusers continue their challenge, He states that the one who is without sin is the one who should cast the first stone. The accusers and congregants depart, realizing that none of them is without sin, leaving Jesus alone with the woman. Jesus asks the woman if anyone has condemned her. She answers that no one has condemned her. Jesus says that He, too, does not condemn her and tells her to go and sin no more.

There is no greater weapon that the enemy uses than guilt, shame, and condemnation. It is more deadly than drinking poison because of how it causes you to self- sabotage. This woman had committed the sin of which she was accused. She was caught in the very act; there was no doubt it was her. They brought her to Jesus in hopes that He would condemn her; however, His response was vastly different. Jesus was about His Father's business: teaching the people the Word of God.

He was interrupted by those who had something so compelling to share that they could not wait. They wanted a stoning this day, after all. That was the penalty for what she had done. She so rightly deserved it, because the law stated such. Jesus tries to ignore them with their accusations. However, they insist that He hears them out.

In the church world, I was taught that you did everything politically correctly. We thrived on the fact that we were doing things correctly. Never, ever, in my mind was I permitted to believe that God would bless me if I didn't do everything right. The realization that I had to come to, after my process, was that there were things that I had not done right, and because I didn't do things right, I felt like God was punishing me. It wasn't until I decided to read this story of this woman caught in adultery, and recently, another book called *The Grace Driven Life*, that I fully began to understand the message of God's grace. I had to really study the pages of each for it to hit home and to embrace the concept called grace. I had never preached or taught on this attribute of God before, but I slowly began to encounter the message it carried. When you constantly believe that God is going to get you and that you're always in trouble with Him, you'll never encounter or experience His grace. You'll literally block yourself off from receiving His goodness.

Reading the Word, praying twenty times a day, or the other things that I may have been erroneously taught was not helping me to get anywhere in my process. I was stuck. When my mindset shifted from performing to receiving God's acceptance and love, I became closer to getting out of my process. I was now seeing what I had been missing out on. I embraced the fact that God loved me-flaws and all.

Many of you are facing situations where the accusations are not false. You are in the throes of scandal, trial, shame, and heartache, just to name a few. People are talking and sharing your failures through text, phone calls, or social media. They are asking that you pay for what you have done. You may be the subject of gossip and the topic of the day. There is no doubt that you are guilty. Your choices may have put you in a place where your relationships may be threatened, or you may be facing a legal situation; whatever the consequences are, you will be all right.

Jesus chooses to ignore the accusers, yet when forced to address the situation, He makes a profound statement: "Let him without sin cast the first stone." Everything gets quiet, and they begin to walk away one at a time. Then he asks the woman, "Woman, where are thine accusers?" She recognizes that the accusers left the scene once they realize that they cannot trap Jesus nor accuse the woman, as they themselves had sinned.

How similar to situations we see in our own lives: people accusing us, when they themselves are guilty. We must embrace the truth that we all have sinned and come short of the glory of God. People in church judge you based on your actions and judge themselves based on their intentions.

We must accept the fact that people are still being processed. Each of us go from glory to glory; we all have areas of weakness. However, to sin means to miss the mark. When we miss the mark, we have an advocate with the Father who is interceding for us daily.

Let's look at how this woman must feel as she is standing before the King of kings and Lord of lords, being accused of something she was caught in the act of doing. She is undeniably guilty, as she was caught in the very act. Everybody has been guilty of something at one point or another in their lives; we must admit that. I can only imagine the intense guilt, fear, and shame that this woman must feel as her accusers surround her, ready to stone her to death. Most people are tempted to lie when they are in such situations; however, this woman just stood there and took it.

When we are faced with accusations and we are guilty, we should take the same position. We should not try to defend our wrong; we should make decisions to accept responsibility for what we have done and ask our loving Father to forgive us. There will always be people who will bring up the area that you failed in, but that is the working of the evil one, trying to shame you and keep you in guilt and condemnation.

When we operate in the spirit of condemnation, we lose our confidence in God. There are so many times when people mistake conviction for condemnation. When we are convicted, the Holy Spirit is grieved with our sin, and it gives us an uneasy feeling about our conduct. Condemnation comes from the enemy, who uses the situation to gain an advantage over the believer. He uses condemnation to keep us from spending time with God. When we yield to God, we will be led away from danger, but condemnation will lead us away from God. Both conviction and condemnation make people grieve over their sin. One leads to life, and the other leads to death. You must treat the spirit of condemnation like the evil it is. That discernment comes from your relationship and communion with God. We must know the difference between the two.

CONDEMNATION

Condemnation can be vague and can leave one feeling hopeless. We can simply feel like something is wrong, but we may not always know why. Condemnation will make you cover your sin and hide from God, just like what happened with Adam and Eve. Condemnation does not point up to Christ and the gospel; rather, it just keeps us meditating and rehearsing in our minds, over and over, the sins we have committed. We know something should change, but we don't know how to make that happen. Adam and Eve did not have the advantage of the Word of God like we have, so they were helpless and clueless as they hid in the garden until God came for them and called them out.

Remember, that condemnation is not your friend; it is hateful and can steal your joy, hurt you, burden you, and not bless you. Condemnation makes you feel hopeless and causes you much emotional pain. Condemnation is always lying to Christians about God and His love for them.

CONVICTION

Conviction is the opposite of condemnation. Conviction is clear, and condemnation feels like a cloud of guilt and shame hovering over you. Conviction may bring a precise thought to your mind, such as *I need to quit watching that show or I should stop gossiping*. It is clear enough to give you a path to move toward repentance, as when David's conscience smote him for cutting Saul's robe, which was as if he was attacking one of God's anointed. When you are convicted, it is loving and correcting to show you a better way. It is a way God uses to get your attention to protect and bless you. We must learn to appreciate God's protection as He corrects those He loves. His correction brings us to a place of repentance and forgiveness, as we see with David in Psalm 32:3-5.

Conviction causes us to know that we are not left alone, but that we can trust the loving Father to forgive us and cleanse us of all unrighteousness. So, if you feel convicted, as you are aware that you are guilty, run to the loving arms of the Savior. Stop beating yourself up over missing the mark. Embrace God's grace to cover you and heal that broken area in your life. When we love Christ we will never intentionally sin, but when we do, we must learn to run to Him and admit what we have done and allow Him to wash it away.

There are always penalties for sin, even though God forgives. We cannot allow ourselves to be deceived into believing that we sin and get away from the penalty. "Be not deceived; God is not mocked: for whatsoever a man soweth, that shall he also reap" (Galatians 6:7

KJV). Think carefully before indulging in sinful behavior, even when you feel weak. Not only do you have the guilt and shame to deal with, you also have the penalty to think about.

Jesus told the woman who was caught in adultery to "go and sin no more." I would consider that a profoundly serious statement. When we refuse to listen to the Holy Spirit when He is nudging us to repent or turn away from harmful behaviors and when we try to handle our own sin, we are inevitability setting ourselves up to sin more. It is a myth to believe that the worse you feel about doing something wrong, it will somehow cause you to slow or stop certain behaviors. With human behavior we tend to increase the behavior. There is no joy in that, and if we are not able to return to joy through repentance, we will ultimately end up sinning more in failed attempts to find joy apart from God.

There Is a Difference Between GUILT and SHAME

Guilt and shame are not the same, even though many people assume the two are interchangeable. They are remarkably similar, but we must know the differences, especially when it comes to understanding how Jesus came to free us from both guilt and shame. We should be godly and sorry for what we do wrong, but never allow shame to take us over. 2 Corinthians 7:10 (NIV) tell us: "Godly sorrow brings repentance that leads to salvation and leaves no regret, but worldly sorrow brings death." This depicts how serious shame is if tolerated in our lives.

The woman caught in adultery could have been so ashamed that she was unable to look up at Jesus, but she stayed and was going to take her punishment. I cannot understand why they never brought the man. He had to also have been caught in the act of adultery. Have you ever been in a situation when more than just you were guilty, but the others tried to bring shame on you because they didn't get caught? If you have, please be encouraged, and know that God is with you and will help you to get through the situation.

Just feeling bad for sin or getting caught is not enough to change behavior, to be forgiven, or to get rid of guilt. It takes godly sorrow—a broken and contrite heart, as outlined in Psalm 51. When we are truly ready as a Christian for change, this is the best prayer to pray; however, if you are living a life of sin, you must pray the prayer to accept Jesus as Lord and Savior, and He will cleanse you.

You can pray this prayer to accept Jesus Christ into your heart:

"Lord Jesus, forgive me for my sin. I believe God raised Jesus Christ from the dead just for me. I accept You as my Lord and my Savior."

Now that you are a new Christian, you should tell somebody! When you accept Jesus, He washes you of all your sins and iniquities. You have no need to feel guilt or shame any longer. You are now a new creation, and old things have passed away; all things are being made new. You are literally in transformation—accept your newfound freedom!

The proper response for conviction is repentance. To repent means to make an about-face. If you are going in one direction, when you repent you go in the other direction. You are now free to start your new life.

If you are a Christian, and you are in sin and need to repent, follow these steps:

- Confess your sin
- If you are holding something against someone, say, "I release and forgive them from my heart."
- Ask God to forgive you
- Receive God's forgiveness by saying, "I receive Your

forgiveness, and I release guilt and shame."
- Receive God's unconditional love for you by saying, "Father, I receive Your love, which is unconditional and complete."
- Commit to turning from sin, and ask God to strengthen and deliver you so that you will no longer have the desire for that thing.

Guilt is a feeling you get when you've done something wrong or perceive you've done something wrong, whereas shame is a feeling that your whole self is wrong, and it may not be related to a specific behavior or event. We can experience both guilt and shame at the same time. Shame is more relational, and it has to do with the feelings of failure when it comes to how others see you and how you perceive yourself. Since it is relational, we can experience it because of our own actions or the actions of others. We can feel shame when we have done nothing wrong at all, but when someone does things to us or something happens to us.

We can live free from shame by standing on the Word of God. In Hebrews 12:2 (MEV) it says, "To Jesus, the author and finisher of our faith, who for the joy that was set before him endured the cross, despising the shame, and is seated at the right hand of the throne of God." Romans 10:11 (ESV) says, "Everyone who believes in him will not be put to shame." Jesus despised the shame of the cross; He was rejected by His friends, disrespected, mocked, and worse, yet He did not allow the shame to stop Him from completing the work because of "the joy that was set before Him." Jesus takes that shame that rightfully belongs to us and covers us when we place our faith in Him. All we must do to access this liberty is to believe.

You must be willing to fight to maintain your liberty. There is an adversary who does not want you to win, but you have the victory. The reason so many Christians hang on to guilt, even though they know about God's total forgiveness, is that the enemy does not want us to be free. He does not want God to have His glory shown through the miracle of forgiveness. He would much rather you walk around with a cloud of guilt and shame. Satan is the father of all of it, and he is constantly lying to you and about you.

The Bible says he is accusing us night and day before the throne of God, in Revelation 12:10. Embracing God's forgiveness may be a theological concept, but it also has practical implications for your daily life. Here are some practical steps that will help you to ensure your victory against this force of shame coming up against you:

1. Recognize the voice of the enemy when he is speaking. You cannot hear God's voice clearly if you do not spend time in the Word and in His presence. The voice of the enemy will try to taunt you, for the purpose of keeping you in bondage. Say this: "I hear the voice of God and resist the voice of Satan."

2. Remember the price Jesus paid for you and speak it out loud. We have all sinned and come short of the glory of God, and if it were not for Jesus' death on the cross, we would be forever condemned by our sin. Say this: "Jesus paid the price for my sin; therefore, I refuse and resist the spirit of shame."

3. Declare truth; you shall know the truth, and the truth shall make you free. Say this: "Satan, I refuse to believe your lies, and I declare that I have total victory in my life in the name of Jesus."

4. Forgive yourself; it is important that you release yourself and accept the fact that you are going from glory to glory. Release yourself from the negative self-talk and begin to say aloud, "I forgive and release myself from the spirit of guilt, shame, and condemnation. I command it to leave my mind, my heart, my spirit, and my atmosphere, in Jesus' name!"

When guilt, shame, or accusations come against you, you can also worship. Like the adulterous woman, you must be able to take the pieces thrown at your life and begin to accept that no matter what you've done, grace says that you belong here. Sing and praise God with all your might. Worship is a wall of protection around your soul. So, you can worship and declare the truths of God's Word.

***

CHAPTER SIX

They Accused Jesus:

He Endured All Accusations
as Part of the Process

Jesus was also named among the accused. He is living proof that every person who will become great in this world will walk through this test. He understood the price He had to pay to fulfill the purpose and plans of God. It is even more clear that the love that He had for the people during His time, and His love for us that would come after Him, is indescribable. He endured all the accusations, punishments, and pain for all of us. Let us explore some of the accusations He had to endure.

Why did Jesus Christ heal on the Sabbath day? The law prohibited Jesus from working on the Sabbath, yet Jesus decided that He would obey God, so He healed the sick and cast out devils. He did not do this to disobey the law, but because He knew God wanted Him to deliver His people.

Let us look at some of those miracles, which will give us a better understanding as to why Jesus would do what He did. Now, let's look at the commandment given by Moses. It is common knowledge that the LORD told Israel in the Ten Commandments, as given through Moses in Exodus 20:8-11 (KJV), "Remember the sabbath day, to keep it holy. Six days shalt thou labour, and do all thy work: But the seventh day is the sabbath of the LORD thy God: in it thou shalt not do any work, thou, nor thy son, nor thy daughter, thy manservant, nor thy maidservant, nor thy cattle, nor thy stranger that is within thy gates: For in six days the LORD made heaven and earth, the sea, and all that in them is, and rested the seventh day: wherefore the

LORD blessed the sabbath day, and hallowed it." This was repeated in Deuteronomy 5:13-15. The Jews were not to work on the Sabbath day at all. In fact, one who picked up sticks on the Sabbath was stoned to death, as God instructed (Numbers 15:32-36)!

It was a violation of the law. Let's look at Matthew 12:1 (KJV): "At that time Jesus went on the sabbath day through the corn; and his disciples were an hungred, and began to pluck the ears of corn and to eat. But when the Pharisees saw it, they said unto him, Behold, thy disciples do that which is not lawful to do upon the sabbath day."

There was purpose in Jesus and what He did on the Sabbath day. Let's discover why: in Matthew 12:10-15, the man with the withered hand had an issue, and Jesus chose to heal him. They asked Him, "Is it lawful for you to heal on the Sabbath?" hoping to accuse Him. His perspective that He was trying to get them to see was: if a sheep falls into a pit, would you leave it, or would you help lift it out? Then He asked, "How much better is a man than a sheep?" He then healed the man.

There are religious people who would rather help a sheep than a man, yet they claim to love Jesus. It is amazing when you decide to follow God and then get attacked, but there are those who would rather accuse than to see humanity healed and free. When these types of things happen to us, we are somewhat taken aback by the behavior. The enemy then tries to use this to get us to back off from the Word of God. He tries to get us to justify healings or deliverances, and we cannot allow this to happen to us. We must press forward, regardless of the attacks of accusation. Once we know that God has told us to move forward with healings, or anything else, we must move forward. We must make the decision that the cost of obeying God will be much more beneficial than our reputation and/or the opinions of men. He was then avidly accused of healing on the Sabbath. They literally held a council against Him, as to how they might destroy Him.

TRUTH OUTLIVES THE LIE

You may feel when you are targeted that it is personal, but it is not personal. It is what happens to every person who has gone where you are going. It is the cost of obedience; it is the price we all must pay. Heal the man!

Let's look at Luke 13:10-16 (KJV). There is a woman who was bowed over, and this infirmity had bound her for eighteen years. Remember, her physical illness symbolizes her spiritual illness (sin nature, captive to Satan). When Jesus saw her, he called to her and said to her, "Woman, thou art loosed from thine infirmity. And he laid his hands on her: and immediately she was made straight, and glorified God" (verses 12-13). You would wonder why they were so furious that He healed her on the Sabbath, when the love of God would cause anyone to want to be free from pain and suffering.

It is another example of what happens when a religious spirit attacks the movement of God. It did not matter to them that this healing was going to glorify God. They said to Him, "There are six days in which men ought to work... not on the sabbath day" (verse 14). Jesus called them hypocrites. He told them, "You know you would rescue your *ass* if he were in trouble on the Sabbath, but you would rather this daughter of Abraham, who has suffered all these years, remain bound?" There are people out there who will crucify you for doing the will of God, even when it glorifies God. My point is to get you to see that the accusations that come against you have nothing to do with the will of God, or whether you are doing something right or wrong. So prepare yourself, as you see the will of God made manifest in your life.

On another Sabbath day, as documented in Luke 14:1-4, Christ healed a man who suffered from dropsy (edema). He asked them the same question about animals and people. He silenced them when he made them reflect by rebuking them. They could not answer him again. Sometimes the only way to silence your accusers is to address them directly. Strong rebuke is sometimes necessary, and this was the case here. This man was suffering and needed to see the healing power of God manifested in his situation. Can you imagine how many people witnessed this miracle and became followers of Christ? I am sure there were untold numbers, but they are not mentioned in the account.

There are untold numbers of people watching you right now. They are watching how you choose to handle the accusations coming against your life. Many may believe the lies and accusations in the beginning, but keep living and obeying God, and He will vindicate you.

We see yet another instance of Jesus Christ healing a lame man on the Sabbath day in John 5:1-16. Let us examine a few of these passages in detail in order to gain a better understanding of why Jesus Christ healed on the Sabbath. Can you imagine being lame or unable to walk, and religious leaders are opposing your healing? It is unthinkable, but it happened years ago, and it happens today. Heal the man and take the hit.

Now, we look at John 5:1-16. In Jerusalem, there was a pool where the mute, the crippled, the blind, and other sick people went to be healed. An angel occasionally came down and stirred the water. The first person to get into the water immediately after the angel came would be made whole (healed). One man sitting beside the pool had been unable to walk for thirty-eight years (verse 5). The Lord Jesus Christ saw the crippled man waiting by the pool, so He asked the sick man if he wanted to be healed. Jesus instantly healed the man (verse 9).

This was on the Sabbath day, so Israel's religious leaders were upset again (verses 9, 16, 18). When the waters are troubled and others do not believe you deserve your miracle, and the spirit of accusation is swirling around, refuse to accept the excuse and press in. Determine to be the first one in the pool; ignore the external chatter. Silence the voice in your head that says, "Look at how long it has been." Press into your healing and past the voice of the accusers.

Let us briefly look at why God established the Sabbath day, and then we will come back to Christ's earthly ministry. The Sabbath is Saturday, and never Sunday in scripture. It is established in Genesis 2:1-3, and after this it is not mentioned again until by Moses, years later. The LORD commanded Israel not to do any work on the Sabbath-they were to rest on the Sabbath (Leviticus 23:3). Instead, every Jew was to spend the Sabbath day thinking about God's purpose in creation and thus, the nation of Israel's role in His plan for the earth (Exodus 31:13-18; Exodus 35:2-3).

So, what was God's purpose in creation when He rested on that first Sabbath back in Genesis chapter 2? Psalm 132:8 (KJV) reads, "Arise, O LORD, into thy rest; thou, and the ark of thy strength." Verses 13 and 14 tell us: "¹³For the LORD hath chosen Zion; he hath desired it for his habitation. ¹⁴This is my rest for ever: here will I dwell; for I have desired it." God's purpose in creating the earth was to set up an earthly kingdom, which He had planned from the time He created the world (Matthew 25:34). Had sin not entered into creation with the fall of Adam and man, God would have come down and lived on planet earth on the Sabbath that followed the first Sabbath of Genesis 2:1-3. This is why God referred to the Promised Land as His "rest" (see Hebrews 3:6-19 and Hebrews 4:1-11). God, in the person of the Lord Jesus Christ, was to come and rest in Israel's land, to enjoy His purpose and plan for creation, for all the work of creation was now finished.

However, we understand that sin interrupted God's plan, and that the earthly kingdom did not come about in Genesis. Instead, beginning with Abram (Abraham) in Genesis chapter 12, God started a new race of people: the nation of Israel. God would make Israel His chosen people on earth. Once saved, the Jews would restore God's authority in the earth (which had been lost when Adam fell, and man's dominion on the earth was passed to Satan; cf. Genesis 1:28; 2 Corinthians 4:4; Galatians 1:4; Ephesians 2:2).

To the nation of Israel God would give that earthly kingdom that He had planned back with Adam and creation (Exodus 19:3-6). When the Jews kept the Sabbath holy every week, they were continually reminded of that earthly kingdom and their role in God's purpose and plan for creating the earth. Unfortunately, Satan polluted the nation of Israel with pagan idolatry and false religion; also, he sent false prophets to mislead Israel, and his evil spirits seduced and possessed Jews (Deuteronomy 13:1-18; Jeremiah 6:13; Acts 8:7-24; Acts 13:6-8; 2 Peter 2:1-3; et al.).

As long as Satan kept Israel in spiritual bondage, the Jews could not be the vessels that God had intended them to be. This continued throughout the Old Testament, whose prophets emphatically preached of Israel's coming kingdom. Finally, Jesus Christ, Israel's King-Redeemer, was born, and He came to usher in their kingdom. However, that earthly kingdom was further postponed when the Jews rejected and crucified Jesus Christ on Calvary's cross. Had Israel accepted Jesus as her Messiah-King 2,000 years ago, that earthly kingdom would have been set up. But that kingdom will not be established until the second coming of Christ, some 6,000 years since creation, and a day beyond even our time!

Israel had forgotten the meaning of the first Sabbath day. By the time Jesus Christ showed up in Matthew, Israel was worshipping the Sabbath instead of worshipping the God of the Sabbath. Israel had no idea what the Sabbath day was all about.

Accusation of Jesus - The Love of His People

John 18:29-30 (ERV)

²⁹*So Pilate went outside to them and asked, "What do you say this man has done wrong?"* ³⁰*They answered, "He is a bad man. That is why we brought him to you."*

There was a trial because of the accusers of Jesus. They accused him of violating the Sabbath law (by healing on the Sabbath), threatening to destroy the Jewish Temple, sorcery, exorcising people by the power of demons, and claiming to be both the Messiah and the Son of God. What an unusual charge. They called him a bad man. Yet he never defended himself. It is truly an experience when you are prosecuted for doing what you were sent to the earth to do. When we are persecuted when we are doing the right thing, it can seem unfair.

Jesus came to the earth for the sole purpose of dying. What a destiny. He lived on the earth for thirty years to prepare for three and a half years of ministry. He had to be processed as our example. We have a first-hand experience by reading about the life of Jesus and His sacrifice for love. There is a price to pay for love. This love cost Jesus His life. He was born of a virgin by a miraculous impregnating, as she answered the angel by saying, "Be it unto me according to thy word" (Luke 1:38 KJV). She truly believed that all things were possible if we could only believe.

The very people Jesus came to die for were the ones who were bringing the accusations against Him. He had taught them and walked among them, yet they despised Him, they rejected Him, and ultimately, they crucified Him.

Most accusations do not compare to what Jesus had to endure. He came to save them and was willing to give His life for the ones that He loved. So, I had to remember that I had to forgive, and love, and choose to release the situation that happened to me. My point is that it hurts when you try to be good to people and they make false accusations against you. It is even more painful when you choose to do as Jesus did and *not say a word.*

In the New Testament, the **Sanhedrin trial of Jesus** refers to the trial of Jesus before the Sanhedrin (a Jewish judicial body) following His arrest in Jerusalem and prior to His dispensation by Pontius Pilate. It is an event reported by all four canonical Gospels of the New Testament, although John's Gospel does not explicitly mention a Sanhedrin trial in this context. Jesus is generally quiet, does not mount a defense, and rarely responds to the accusations, but is condemned by the Jewish authorities for various accusations. The Jewish leaders then take Jesus to Pontius Pilate, the governor of Roman Judaea, and ask that He be tried for claiming to be the King of the Jews.

The trial, as depicted in the synoptic gospels, is temporally placed informally on Thursday night, and then again formally on Friday morning. However, since the Jewish preparation day begins Thursday at sunset, according to the Gospel of John this informally happened Wednesday night, and then again formally on Thursday morning, with Him eventually being taken off the cross Thursday night, that being the beginning of the Jews' "day of preparation," as it is written in John 19:42.

We know that they chose to release another prisoner when Pilate gave them the chance to release a prisoner. He was destined to die. If He had not died, we would not have an opportunity to be saved and to have a personal relationship with our heavenly Father. They crucified the Lord of glory, having no earthly idea that it was the perfect will of God. It was His divine plan to redeem mankind back unto Himself.

Many times, we are persecuted and allowed to suffer because of the people connected to us that He wants to save. Our lives are never about just ourselves, but other people—especially when we are called of God to the ministry. You will pay a price for the people and the anointing you carry to set them free. Many times, you will find yourself accused of things that you had no idea you would be accused of doing.

In these three examples we see that loss, ministry, and callings are all very precious to God, and they require processing. This process will cause everything that is not like God to come off of your life so that you remain pure and uncontaminated by what you have had to go through.

It is going to take the Word and much prayer to be free. These are different from the various types of accusations we will eventually cover.

Jesus Christ, "The Son of Man" and "Lord of the Sabbath Day": His Sabbath-Day Miracle-Ministry Explained

On three occasions, Jesus Christ called Himself "The Son of Man, Lord of the Sabbath Day" (Matthew 12:8; Mark 2:28; Luke 6:5). What did He mean? He meant that He had ordained that first Sabbath day of Genesis 12:1-3. He knew the significance of the Sabbath—that it was established to glorify Him instead of merely to provide Israel's religious leaders with a nice law to observe and feel pious about. He was saying that Israel's religious leaders had no idea what Sabbath-day worship really was! Jesus Christ was the perfect Man, "the Son of Man," as opposed to sinful Adam or sinful Israel, for He was the Man who would accomplish Father God's original intention in creation. Jesus Christ was also the LORD God manifest in human flesh, the Person whom creation was to glorify (Colossians 1:16-20).

We thus understand why Jesus Christ healed on the Sabbath day. When Israel's Messiah and King (Jesus) came, as documented in the Bible books of Matthew, Mark, Luke, and John, there was a spike in the number of devil- possessed and sick Jews. As long as Israel was in spiritual darkness and satanic bondage, God could not use them in their kingdom to evangelize Gentiles. Do you remember the woman in Luke 13:16 (KJV), whom we briefly discussed earlier? "And ought not this woman, being a daughter of Abraham, whom Satan hath bound, lo, these eighteen years, be loosed from this bond on the sabbath day?"

That physically crippled woman was spiritually impotent Israel, firmly bound by Satan's chains and spiritually blind! The Jews were to be released from that satanic bondage on the Sabbath, the millennial (1000-year) reign of Christ, the period of "rest" that the Saturday Sabbath typified.

Notice what Mark 5:10 (KJV) says: "And he [the unclean spirit] besought him [the Lord Jesus Christ] much that he would not send them away out of the country." The devils did not want to be cast out of "the country." They did not want to be cast out of the land of Israel! Furthermore, the devils rightly claimed that Jesus Christ had come to destroy them by setting up His kingdom and binding them. The Lord Jesus Christ told the Jews whom He healed that their sins were forgiven (Matthew 9:2; Mark 2:5; Luke 5:20; Luke 7:48). Jesus was casting out devils and healing all manner of disease and sickness and preaching "the gospel of the kingdom" (Matthew 9:35; cf. Matthew 4:17).

He also sent out His twelve apostles to heal and preach "the gospel of the kingdom" (Matthew 10:1-8). The Lord Jesus was demonstrating to Israel the healing, prosperity, and forgiveness that God would provide for the Jews during their earthly kingdom. The "binding of the strong man" is Jesus Christ casting Satan out of Israel's midst (Matthew 12:24-32; Mark 3:22-30; Luke 11:15-26).

Notice Matthew 12:15 (KJV), which occurred right after the healing of the man with the withered hand (recall that it was on the Sabbath). "But when Jesus knew it, he withdrew himself from thence: and great multitudes followed him, and he healed them all." Here is an example of Jesus healing multitudes of people on the Sabbath. This healed multitude also symbolized Israel being healed in her earthly kingdom.

Jesus Christ was not only healing Israel physically, but spiritually as well. Every time Christ cast out a devil (unclean spirit), He was diminishing Satan's influence over the nation of Israel. Interestingly, the crippled man in John 5:5 had been handicapped for thirty-eight years. Amazingly, Deuteronomy 2:14 says that Israel wandered in the wilderness for thirty-eight years. During that period, the Jews were rebellious and spiritually crippled and unable to enter the Promised Land, the earthly kingdom of Jesus Christ.

When Jesus healed the man suffering from dropsy in Luke 14:1-4, recall that He healed him too on the Sabbath day. This sick man also symbolized Israel, spiritually impotent and under Satan's control. Again, by healing the sick, especially on the Sabbath day, Jesus was demonstrating to the Jews that their earthly kingdom would bring spiritual and physical healing. The man whose withered hand was healed on the Sabbath (Matthew 12:10-15; Mark 3:1-6; Luke 6:6-11) also symbolized Israel's physical and spiritualhealing in her coming kingdom.

An example of one being devil-possessed is the man possessed by the unclean spirit in Mark 1:21-27 and Luke 4:31-36. Notice that the unclean spirit asked Jesus (Mark 1:24; Luke 4:34 KJV): "Let us alone; what have we to do with thee, thou Jesus of Nazareth? art thou come to destroy us? I know thee who thou art, the Holy One of God." The devil knew exactly what Christ was there to do. Christ was there to destroy Satan's stronghold on this person. He was here to bring in the kingdom that the Sabbath day had shadowed for some time. How could anyone know that a person was demon possessed and take issue with healing him on Sabbath? Jesus obeyed God and took responsibility for the consequences.

The Pharisees and scribes had such a religious mindset that they completely missed the point of why Jesus Christ was healing on the Sabbath. Hence, they accused Him of being a "blasphemer" and a "law-breaker." They were so preoccupied with keeping the Sabbath (vain religious tradition) that they had lost sight of why God had implemented Sabbath-day keeping in the first place.

Additionally, they completely missed the point that by performing those miracles, Jesus was proving that He was their Messiah. However, these religious leaders had wicked hearts of unbelief, and they used anything to discredit Jesus Christ and thus accused Him of Sabbath-day breaking.

They did not have hearts of faith or spiritual eyes to see the meaning of those Sabbath-day miracles of Christ. In their hypocrisy, these unbelievers had totally missed the fact that they broke the Sabbath when they circumcised a male Jew on the Sabbath when it was the eighth day (John 7:22-24). Even today, Bible critics complain that Jesus Christ broke the Sabbath day on many occasions-they too have no idea what the Sabbath day means, or they would not utter such rash comments, which is why this chapter is so important.

While the Sabbath day was important, it was a ceremonial law. Sometimes, the Sabbath day needed to be broken (such as in the case of physical circumcision). Furthermore, Jesus Christ spoke of losing or helping animals on the Sabbath (Matthew 12:11,12; Luke 14:5); Moses made provisions for such actions on the Sabbath (see Exodus 23:5; Deuteronomy 22:4). As to not infringe on other aspects of the Mosaic Law, the Sabbath day would need to be broken-these laws took preeminence above the Sabbath-keeping, because they were the right things to do. Yet the religious leaders of Israel did not want to admit that Jesus healing on the Sabbath was good and acceptable. They were cold and heartless, as religionists are today. They would rather have sick people remain ill than disobey a church law. There are many people today who have become desensitized to the real purpose of Christ.

When Jesus and His disciples were passing through a grain field and His hungry disciples ate some of the crops, the Pharisees complained that they were working on the Sabbath. One of the questions Jesus asked the Pharisees was the following excerpt from Matthew 12:5-8 (KJV): "⁵Or have ye not read in the law, how that on the sabbath days the priests in the temple profane the sabbath, and are blameless? ⁶But I say unto you, That in this place is one greater than the temple. ⁷But if ye had known what this meaneth, I will have mercy, and not sacrifice, ye would not have condemned the guiltless. 8For the Son of man is Lord even of the sabbath day."

The Lord Jesus explained that certain activities had preeminence to Sabbath-day rest, and two of them were having compassion on the hungry (David and his men eating the shewbread; Matthew 12:3-4) and the priests of Israel having to offer sacrifices on the Sabbath. Even Israel's priests had to break the Sabbath day. We saw earlier how they circumcised male Jewish babies on the Sabbath. It is interesting that when people break laws, they try to accuse you of the same exact things.

In Numbers 28:3 (KJV), JEHOVAH commanded Israel through Moses, "This is the offering made by fire which ye shall offer unto the Lord; two lambs of the first year without spot day by day, for a continual burnt offering."

Every day, no matter what day it was, these two lambs were to be offered-one lamb in the morning, and the other lamb in the evening. Even on the Sabbath day, JEHOVAH said, the priests were to minister in the Tabernacle or Temple in this manner.

The priests were to work in the Tabernacle or Temple on the Sabbath. Verses 9-10 (KJV) discuss special offerings that were also to be offered on the Sabbath day: "⁹And on the sabbath day two lambs of the first year without spot, and two tenth deals of flour for a meat offering, mingled with oil, and the drink offering thereof: ¹⁰This is the burnt offering of every sabbath, beside the continual burnt offering, and his drink offering."

In addition to their daily routine, the priests had two more burnt offerings to sacrifice on the Sabbath day. Notice how JEHOVAH gave Israel's priesthood permission to infringe upon Sabbath-day keeping: the priests could not rest on the Sabbath, otherwise they would disobey other commandments of JEHOVAH.

In conclusion, why did Jesus heal on the Sabbath day? He did it to demonstrate "the powers of the world to come" (Hebrews 2:3-5; Hebrews 6:4-6). The Old Testament prophesied that when God would come, the lame man would leap, the mute would sing, the blind would see, and the deaf would hear (Isaiah 35:4-6). When the Messiah would come, there would be no unclean spirits in Israel's land (Zechariah 13:1-2). By performing the healing miracles, especially on the Sabbath, Jesus Christ was fulfilling what the Old Testament had prophesied.

The Jews needed signs and wonders before they would believe God, and Christ's miracles taught Israel what He was going to do with them (Exodus 4:1-8; John 4:48; 1 Corinthians 1:22). Now you know why the Lord Jesus Christ healed on the Sabbath. So, the accusations were unfounded, yet they were still made.

When I wrote this chapter, I thought, *If Jesus was accused, and I have been accused, I should probably do what Jesus did.* As He was receiving the stripes on His back and a crown of thorns upon His head, He exhibited a level of discipline to still look at his accusers with love, praying for them. That is the ultimate high road to take. I must admit that I have not always taken that approach, and it has taken me some time to get to a season where I can do like Jesus did. I often have to remind myself that I can operate in a certain manner, and sometimes I even have to go back and apologize, to correct something I may have said or done that wasn't the appropriate response. Although people may hurt us, we have to give ourselves permission to let the pain of that hurt go. Jesus was divine, but He was also human. It is my desire to be as much like Jesus as I can possibly be. It was after Jesus fulfilled His assignment of forgiveness that He was able to be exalted and glorified in His right standing with God. The message here is simple: we should remember that we too have faults, but the stigma of our past doesn't disqualify us from being recipients of God's unmerited and unwavering grace.

***

CHAPTER SEVEN

The Courts of Heaven:

The Place Where Everything Changes

Psalm 100:4-5 (KJV)

⁴Enter into his gates with thanksgiving, and into his courts with praise: be thankful unto him, and bless his name. ⁵For the Lord is good; his mercy is everlasting; and his truth endureth to all generations.

Many Christians are oblivious to the Courts of Heaven. They have not so much as heard that there is such a thing. There are courts in heaven, and the Lord is good, and His mercy endures forever! I had to listen to a lot of teaching and study to present this information. It is in no way a conclusive study on the Courts of Heaven, but an introduction and steps that will help you to wage effective warfare.

In order to advance to the next level in your life, you must master the current level you are at and learn how to break through. This new level is nothing like the levels before. This is the reason why the last season of your life was so difficult. Nothing you were able to use in the past was enough to break this current level of opposition, and you are now forced to increase in your knowledge, strategy, and understanding.

My personal story includes a spiritual plateau, and me not understanding what I was up against, and how the opposition was preparing me for the next thing God had for me. Everything I had known to do was not working. Every strategy that had worked in the past was not working and was not moving the opposition and resistance that was current. Every area of my life was under attack. I thought I understood spiritual warfare—and I believe I did, for the level I was on—but for where I was going, I was unprepared.

My family, finances, ministry, and relationship were taking a terrible beating. There were things coming against me that I had not experienced before. Every prayer group, intercessor, and direction was closed. I could get a prophecy with a date, and the date would go by and there was no manifestation. If it were just one every now and again, I'd blame it on the prophets. But when there are three or more giving you prophetic words and dates and none of them are coming to pass, you must re-focus and re-align, because somehow you are the common denominator. That was me, in the midst of every storm imaginable, and I was trying to use old methods and I was failing. Then the accusations increased by astronomical numbers, and from everywhere you could imagine. Sometimes I believed the devil would whisper lies into the atmosphere, and people would just pick them up and repeat them as truths against me and my life.

I was forced to accept the fact that I could not respond and win. I had to learn to bear the burden of increase and expansion. I had to encourage others not to take offense at what people were saying and accusing me of. I had to encourage them and go home and cry myself into the loving arms of Jesus. I had to pray for my heart to be protected from revenge and/or retaliation. Even though I realized that I had to learn to silence my accusers by using the method and strategy that God was teaching me.

One of my most admired preachers posted this on social media, and it rang so true concerning my journey: "Tonight, I'm studying the psychological power of an identity crisis. One of the consequences of not recovering from a hard season in the way you should is that your grip on your personal identity is not as firm as it used to be. If you're not careful, a storm, a trial, a test, or a time of transition and change will make you forget (or simply not like) who God made you to be."

- Dr. Matthew L. Stevenson III.

This attack and trial left me disillusioned and despondent. I forgot who I was and could not envision who I was to become. Psychologically, I was experiencing a spiritual identity crisis. If you have experienced divorce, or any other major traumatic experience that altered your entire lifestyle, and you have not prepared properly, I am a living witness that your personal identity will be flawed and filtered through the rubbish of your attack. I literally did not even know which last name to use, or what I was really called to do. Many attacks back-to-back, unreal circumstances, and pressure in ways unimaginable—and as soon as I started to recover, another hidden enemy would expose themselves.

In this type of transition you should give all of your friends a pass, because you may soon discover that they were not your friends at all. They were with you for other motives; they used you, they abused you, and then they lied on you. The very ones you took off the street, and provided for and protected, twisted everything that was done and used it to join the other executioners. While we all make mistakes, and some things we may very well be guilty of, they used your good intentions and tried to categorize you. All of these spirits will come up against you simultaneously while you are trying to recover.

Interestingly, in my case the Lord removed most every person I would go to for prayer and counseling and started to choose the people for me. There were mostly older, more mature believers that God surrounded me with. Those who could pray, love, and see the truth of what was happening. God placed me in the loving care of midwives who had been tried and tested. They were not interested in what I could offer; they wanted me to *outlive the lies*. You could tell them anything you wanted to about me and they were steadfast, non-judgmental, and full of the love of God. The people that you run to because they are popular are not always pure. They struggle with jealousy and secret hate for you, and it all comes out when they choose to believe the lies.

Through it all, God causes you to face the giants of accusation and disdain as you enter the room. It is not to punish you, but to build you and to teach you how to overcome the accusations and options of others and to keep your character intact. Now, for a warrior, that is torture. Warriors want to go to war. But when God is breaking the old and trying to introduce you to the new, you make a decision to bear the pain by resisting the flesh and submitting to God.

The greatest thing that happened for me in this part of my journey is that I could begin to recognize new people who were coming into my life who had similar characteristics. It taught me to recognize and choose better. So, I started this massive release party. Anybody who came along that demonstrated the toxicity of the other people who had lied and accused me, I would disconnect and begin to search for others who had the characteristics that I wanted to emulate in my life. Toxic people will keep you toxic and filled with issues. Disconnect early and spare yourself new testimonies.

All of my testimony brings me to the Courts of Heaven, because it was not until I discovered this truth that I was able to break free from the stuck place I found myself in. I was able to understand so many things about myself and who I am really. I trust that this part of my book will liberate you more and more as you read. This is where I found my freedom!

When I was faced with my son possibly getting life in prison, God gave me a strategy, and I presented it before the Courts of Heaven. During my time of praise and worship, I would make this declaration: "God will deliver those for whom we intercede who are not innocent, by the cleanness of our hands." That was the word that

I fought with. After two years of believing what I had declared, my son was adjudicated as a juvenile and the court placed him in my care and ordered that he get his college degree. I won in victory because I submitted my case in the Courts of Heaven and declared the strategies of God to be manifested in my son's case here on the earth.

Remember chapter 1, when Job was considered. The enemy considered Job, and then he accused him in the throne room of God. The Courts of Heaven operate like the legal system we see on the earth. God is constantly releasing new information about this revelation; again, read this as an introduction. Jesus Himself shed His blood for us, and it has been sprinkled on the mercy seat. Jesus carried a cross, and it was our verdict—but we must understand that the will of God is not automatic; therefore, we must enforce this by entering into the justice system of God. We access the Courts of Heaven through prayer and intimacy with Jesus.

Let's look at several different types of courts mentioned in the Word of God that I discovered in my studies:

- Court of Mediation - the word *mediation* means to have an intervention in a dispute in order to resolve it; arbitration. It literally means to settle outside of court. This should be the first step in the process. Mediation is a sort of reconciliation. *Reconciliation* means the restoration of friendly relations, which causes us to examine ourselves to ensure that we are in right relationship with God. That there is nothing giving the enemy legal rights or access into your life to keep a curse operative. 2 Corinthians 5:18 (NKJV), *"Now all things are of God, who has reconciled us to Himself through Jesus Christ, and has given us the ministry of reconciliation."*

- Court of Petition - the word *petition* means a formal, written request, typically one signed by many people, appealing to authority with respect to a particular cause. Once we examine ourselves and our hearts, the next step we would like to take is to petition God, asking God for the things that have been promised to us in His Word. We bring prayers and petitions with thanksgiving. Philippians 4:6 (NIV): *"Do not be anxious about anything, but in every situation, by prayer and petition, with thanksgiving, present your requests to God."* We must decide to be thankful, even when we are being falsely accused, and to give God thanks and refuse to be anxious or worry.

- Throne of Grace - Hebrews 4:16 (KJV): *"Let us therefore come boldly unto the throne of grace, that we may obtain mercy, and find grace to help in time of need."* The throne room of God can be found in the courts, where we have legal rights to a ratified covenant. Psalm 100 says to enter His courts with praise. If in the midst of your situation you can find a way to give God praise, you will find yourself in the court room of Almighty God, where Jesus is seated at His right side to help you to navigate through the accusations of your life. We enter the throne room knowing that God is filled to overflowing with grace and love for every person who will come. We need to know and have the love of God in our hearts (1 John 4:8).

- Court of Mount Zion - In my studies, I discovered that the Throne of Grace and the Court of Petition are linked to a court system similar to the one we have in our western society. Mount Zion is considered the city of the living God, the heavenly Jerusalem. This is the place where thousands of angels are worshipping God, filled in a joyful place. This is the place where you come to God and to Jesus, the mediator of the new covenant and the blood that speaks of a better word even than that which was spoken during the time of

Abel (Hebrews 12:22-24). Throughout the Word of God, Mount Zion is the place of God's justice and judgment. This best describes the Courts of Heaven and how we can approach the Lord.

- Court of the Accuser – Amazingly, there are several scriptures that show Satan accusing people in the courts. Revelation 12:10-11 (KJV): *"¹⁰And I heard a loud voice saying in heaven, Now is come salvation, and strength, and the kingdom of our God, and the power of his Christ: for the accuser of our brethren is cast down, which accused them before our God day and night. ¹¹And they overcame him by the blood of the Lamb, and by the word of their testimony; and they loved not their lives unto the death."* This is the place of accusation; however, it is also the place where testimonies should be given. Day and night we are being accused, and it is especially important for us not to operate in the court of the accuser. That we would not be one that stays before God, accusing others. We will not let Satan use us, but we will not allow him to accuse us. This is the place for the believer to operate in love, forgiveness, and reconciliation.

- Court of the Ancient of Days, or the Supreme Court - the US Supreme Court is the highest court in the land. It is the place where the most important cases are tried. It is the place where laws are explained and enforced. The Supreme Court functions as a last-resort tribunal. Its rulings cannot be appealed. It also decides on cases dealing with the interpretation of the constitution (for example, it can overturn a law passed by Congress if it deems it unconstitutional). *"⁹As I looked, thrones were set in place, and the Ancient of Days took his seat... ¹⁰The court was seated,and the books were opened"* (Daniel 7:9-10 NIV). This is the highest-level court, and you cannot go in. You can be taken in through visions and dreams, but this is not a place to present your case. This is the place where you get verdicts, understand the books that were written about you, and enforce the judgment written.

There are other Courts of Heaven that require greater understanding to operate in, but these are the basic ones that are safe to operate in:

- The Court of Petition

- The Throne of Grace

- The Court of Mount Zion

- The Court of Mediation

Always ask the Lord's permission before operating in the Courts of Heaven. Remember to mediate your case first and settle outside of the Courts of Heaven whenever possible.

For more insight and revelation on the Courts of Heaven- including how to open a case for yourself or a loved one-I encourage you to pray, seek God, and study this topic for more in-depth revelation and understanding.

7 Steps to Overcoming the Spirit of Accusation

1.Find scripture to stand on

Standing on scripture is pivotal to the success of every believer. The Bible teaches us that heaven and earth will pass away, but the Word of God will not pass away. The Word is infallible truth and cannot be resisted by any enemy force. The Word combats many of the forces that are fighting against your destiny. The more Word you can stand on, the more you will believe. Faith comes by hearing, and hearing by the Word of God. War with the Word.

2.Make daily confessions

There is so much power in your words. The power of life and death is in your tongue, or in your words. Your words matter. They are spirit and life, and they are procuring something in the world and in your life. The Bible says that the worlds were framed by the Word of God; therefore, we have that same creative power. If you do not like the way your world is going, change it by the words you say.

3.Find prayer partners

The Bible says that if two of three shall agree on earth, they are going to see things begin to happen. We also know that one can put a thousand opposing forces to flight, and two, ten thousand. So, it is imperative to get reinforcements fighting with you.

4.Control your thinking

We must take note of the thoughts we are thinking. We are admonished to think on things that are good, pure, and lovely, and of a good report; we are to put on the mind of Christ, and we must be transformed by renewing our mind. So, where your mind goes, your life follows. If you are planning to win this war in life, you must win the war in your mind.

5.Plan your comeback

This is much easier said than done. You must maintain a healthy vision of who you are and what you are called to do. I had to put up pictures of myself in ministry to remind me of what I was called to do because of the oblivious railing accusations that were coming up against me. Part of my comeback was to believe that there were endorsers out there whom God would bring into my life who would give me an opportunity or a chance to do what I was born to do.

6.Get a lawyer (the Holy Spirit is our mediator on the earth, and Jesus is our mediator in heaven)

The enemy is going to try to do what he can to keep you ignorant and ill-informed of his tactics. He does not want you to know that Jesus pleads your case as your advocate before the Father. The Holy Spirit is your advocate on the earth. He talks to men on your behalf. You will need both, because you will be accused both in the heavenlies and on the earth. Be of good cheer, because you win!

7.Accusation—Satan has lost—and execute the judgment written

You have every right to remind Satan of his defeat. You must maintain a winning attitude, even when it looks like God has gone on vacation. There were times when people would say, "It is darkest before the dawn," and then my life would get even darker. I thought there was no deeper low that I could go to—but yes, there was, and I went there. I refused to give up. I knew that there was something I was missing, and I had to find it. I knew that Satan was a defeated foe, and his power was not more powerful than the power of God. I stand today to declare that my great God is the most powerful being on the earth, and I will enforce the kingdomand continue to stand against the unfruitful works of darkness.

In conclusion, these were the seven steps I had to use to break the glass ceiling of accusations and to silence the avenger. I had to step it up, and I would like to say that I decided to pray and ask the Lord what was written about me in the scrolls or books in heaven. He directed me to listen to the prophecies that had been spoken over my life. They became my prayers and a part of my winning strategy, as God asked me to look for similarities and to focus on desires and dreams hidden deep within my heart. He said, "That is what is written; they keep telling you through prophecies." This literally liberated me from the opinions of men and the people who were trying to define me, but they are found in the presence of God. What does the book say about you? Say that, and only that!

In these witnesses there is proof that there are books written about you:

Psalm 139:16-17 (NASB)

[16]*Your eyes have seen my unformed substance; and in your book (scroll) were all written the days that were ordained for me, when as yet there was not one of them.* [17]*How precious are your thoughts to me, O God! How vast is the sum of them!*

Psalm 139:16-17 (NLT)

[16]*You saw me before I was born. Every day of my life was recorded in your book. Every moment was laid out before a single day had passed.* [17]*How precious are your thoughts about me, O God. They cannot be numbered!*

Psalm 139:16 (KJV)

Thine eyes did see my substance, yet being unperfect; and in thy book all my members were written, which in continuance were fashioned, when as yet there was none of them.

Psalm 40:7 (KJV)

Then said I, Lo, I come: in the volume of the book it is written of me.

Revelation 20:12 (NKJV)

And I saw the dead, small and great, standing before God, and books were opened. And another book was opened, which is the Book of Life. And the dead were judged according to their works, by the things which were written in the books.

***

CHAPTER EIGHT

The Closing Argument:

Verdict – CASE DISMISSED

Have you ever been falsely accused or lied about? If you have been wrongfully blamed or misunderstood for your intentions, turn to scripture and the power of prayer. Regarding false accusations, the psalmist says, "For they do not speak peace, but against those who are quiet in the land they devise words of deceit" (Psalm 35:20 ESV). This is an accurate description of the motives and results of false accusations. People lie about the innocent in order to stir up trouble.

People accuse others falsely as a revenge tactic, a power play, or when they think they have something to gain. This behavior is unbiblical; moreover, we should respond in a godly way. It's important that we pray and trust God during a period of false accusation and loneliness. While it may not change your circumstances, it will stabilize your spirit. Always remember that you have a basis for confidence, since God Himself is righteous. In the end, His justice and fair play will abound toward you as well. Here are six prayers for the wrongfully blamed.

The Bible tells us, "Above all else, guard your heart, for it is the wellspring of life" (Proverbs 4:23 NIV). We desperately need that reminder when we're wrongfully blamed and under attack. Let's face it—unless we guard our own heart, we will soon be down in the gutter with our opponents. We will be tempted to attack them as they have attacked us, to vilify them, to smear their reputation, and in general to do whatever we have to do to get even with them. It's frightening how quickly we can fall into attack mode when we get angry at heart. But there's hope in God. If you want to turn your heart around, pray this prayer: "Dear Loving God, thank You for another day of life. Today, I seek a change of heart. I was wrongfully blamed for something, and it weighs heavily on my heart. Today, I seek a change of heart. I suffer from my hardness. Please change me, Lord. I know that only You can do this. Amen."

It is possible that in our haste to defend ourselves, we will talk too much, too soon, and with too much emotion. There are times when we need to speak the truth, and in those moments, we must speak truth in love. State the facts, lay out the truth as you see it; don't presume to judge another person's heart, even if they are unfairly judging yours, and don't say anything in a heated moment that you will regret later.

If you are ready to speak the truth as graciously as possible, pray this prayer: "Dear Lord, has it come to this? Is there any chance at all? Or is all hope lost? Please show me, Lord, once again, as You have in days past. Show me, Lord, Your power and Your glory. May Your Spirit fill my spirit. Let me rise up again and be strong in Christ, for I know all control is Yours alone. Amen."

Remember this: you can't control what people do to you or what they say about you. Technology has made it too easy to say whatever we want and then post it on Facebook or YouTube or on a discussion board, regardless of the truth. Our challenge must be to guard our own hearts. In almost all situations, when you are falsely accused, the truth of God's point of view will be more than what you see or what your critics see. And God's will always goes beyond our limited field of vision.

What you want is the truth to be told and God's will to be done. If you're looking for a prayer that is focused on the Lord, not on you or your accusers, turn to this simple prayer: "Dear Lord, let the truth come out, and let Your will be done. I pray that I will keep my focus on You and You alone. Amen."

Don't be surprised when you're falsely accused. We won't always get along with our brothers and sisters in Christ, and these same brothers and sisters may not have your best interests at heart. This is clear when you look at

Ephesians. In Ephesians 3, we receive a reminder that God is able to do far beyond anything we could ask or imagine. When we turn to chapter 4, the first thing out of his mouth is: "Always be humble and gentle. Patiently put up with each other and love each other" (Ephesians 4:2 CEV). Sometimes, people hear what they want to hear regardless of the facts. We should not be overly surprised when, despite our best efforts, our actions are criticized and our motives are questioned.

If you are open and ready to pray for the person who accused you, pray this simple prayer: "Dear God, if I hurt others, give me the strength to apologize. If people hurt me, give me the strength to forgive. Amen."

All those who are falsely accused will feel like the victim at some point. You know you're in victim mode when you feel wronged, used by your friends, involved in unfair accusations, and like you can't get your side of the story fairly told. You also know you're hooked by what was said about you when you can't stop talking about it, you become consumed with the issue, you lose all focus, and you start doing foolish things. When you're in this headspace, you end up frustrated and miserable and nothing is solved.

If you're ready to fight against becoming a victim, pray this prayer: "Dear Lord, today I feel weary and worn. I want to obey You, but I have clung desperately to hope and still feel hopeless. Please strengthen my heart today; renew Your vision for my life and the joy of my salvation. I fix my eyes on You and look to You alone for my help, my hope, my strength, and my deliverance. Amen."

The psalmist says, "The LORD is my strength and my shield; in him my heart trusts, and I am helped; my heart exults, and with my song I give thanks to him" (Psalm 28:7 ESV). When you're wrongfully blamed, it's important that you trust in God to keep you secure and free, for God is our strength and shield. If you're ready for God to help you find security and freedom in Him alone, turn to this prayer: "Heavenly Father, I may not understand why some people do the things they do or how everything will work out, but I trust You. I don't see a way, but I know You will make a way. I have faith at this very moment that You are touching hearts, opening doors, and lining up the right breaks and opportunities. Things may look dark and bleak now, but I have faith that my dawn is coming. Amen."

Those who make false accusations are under God's judgment. The Bible tells us, "You destroy those who speak lies; the LORD abhors the bloodthirsty and deceitful man" (Psalm 5:6 ESV). As followers of Christ, we can expect that people will sometimes make false accusations, but hear Jesus' encouragement: "Blessed are you when people... falsely say all kinds of evil against you because of me. Rejoice and be glad, because great is your reward in heaven" (Matthew 5:11-12 EHV). No matter what others say about us falsely, we can rely on God's Word and trust that God will be beside us to get us through every trial.

Have you ever been falsely accused? Been the subject of gossip? Had lies spread about you? When you know deep in your heart that you are innocent, it is incredibly painful to hear rumors about yourself. To have your integrity brought into question, your reputation slandered. Some days, it is all you can do to get out of bed in the morning, knowing the battle you face. Some days, you simply cry out to God, "Vindicate me, oh God!" *Vindicate.* Clear my name of false accusations. Prove my innocence through the truth. Present evidence justifying my actions. Defend me!

You've probably been there before. I know I have. And I'm walking this path again, hearing my name slandered. I find myself begging God to vindicate me, to make my righteousness shine like the dawn and the justice of my cause like the noonday sun (Psalm 37:6).

I woke up early this morning, after a dream of my accusers coming against me. In my dream, I stood up to those spreading lies against me only to again be made the villain instead of the victim. My heart was racing and the tears stung my eyes as I cried out to God, "Vindicate me! Bring the truth to light! Be my Defender!"

How do we respond to these lies? How do we escape this vicious cycle of attack? How do we survive an evil attack against our name and our reputation? Unjust attacks seem to be the common experience of humanity. A quick search of scripture finds many instances of the words "vindicate me," words typically cried out in the anguish of heart that comes with unjust attacks.

Perhaps King David cried out to God for vindication more often than any other Biblical character. As I search the Psalms, I find some keys to surviving these attacks.

Examine my life

"Test me, Lord, and try me, examine my heart and my mind; for I have always been mindful of your unfailing love and have lived in reliance on your faithfulness" (Psalm 26:2- 3 NIV). Before we can expect God to vindicate us, we must first make sure we are truly innocent of the accusations. We must allow God to search our hearts, to convict us of any sin we might be harboring in our hearts.

In Psalm 17, David stands before God, proclaiming his innocence. He is able to move forward with a clear conscience, knowing he has walked in God's ways. He stands before God clear of any wrongdoing. Have you allowed God to test your heart, to see if there is any truth in the attacks? If you have been found innocent by God, then move forward, head held high.

Trust His protection

"Have mercy on me, my God, have mercy on me, for in you I take refuge. I will take refuge in the shadow of your wings until the disaster has passed" (Psalm 57:1 NIV). Throughout scripture, God promises to be our protector, our refuge in times of trouble (Psalm 59:16). He is our hiding place (Psalm 32:7), the God who saves us (Psalm 88:1), and the rock in whom we take refuge (Psalm 18:2).

God has promised to protect us from harm. Yes, we may face false accusations on this earth. We may deal with unjust attacks. We may feel as if we are going to drown, as if our lives are over.

But the truth is found in scripture: He is our Defender, our protection. The waves of slander may rock us and toss us all about, but He will not let them drown us. If we cling to Him for our protection, we will not be moved.

Trust His character

"I will bow down toward your holy temple and will praise your name for your unfailing love and your faithfulness, for you have so exalted your solemn decree that it surpasses your fame" (Psalm 138:2 NIV). Unfailing love. Faithful. Gracious. Merciful. Forgiving. Slow to anger. Kind. Giver of peace. Fiercely jealous. Infinitely wise. Holy. Sovereign. Good. Infinite, eternal, and incomprehensible. All-powerful and all-knowing. God's character is fully trustworthy, and He is unable to change that character.

God is all-knowing. He knows the truth. He is all- seeing. He sees your pain and the injustice with which you are being treated. He is the one who reveals truth, bringing deeds done in darkness out into the light (1 Corinthians 4:5).

It may not be today. It may not be tomorrow. Or next week, or next month, or even next year. But God's ways are perfect, higher than ours. We can trust His character, trust that He will bring the truth to light. In His faithful love and mercy, He will care for you and sustain you.

Trust His past faithfulness

"*For I have always been mindful of your unfailing love and have lived in reliance on your faithfulness*" (Psalm 26:3 NIV). Throughout scripture, we see people continuously reflecting on God's faithfulness. Whether it's the Israelites reflecting on the Red Sea and the many miracles they experienced in the wilderness, or David reflecting on how God preserved His life from King Saul, or Jacob reflecting on God's goodness at the end of His life (Genesis 48:15), it was a recurring theme to focus on the ways God had walked faithfully with them throughout their lives.

Reflecting on God's past faithfulness reminds us of how He has seen us through in the past, giving us strength to keep moving forward in the present. His nature never changes.

Praise His name

Because of the blood of Jesus, all of your accusers are silenced as long as you enforce your rights! Your case has been *dismissed*.

My Prayer for Today

Lord, give me the attitude that turns every attack the devil sends into an opportunity for revival! Help me to walk in such strong and consistent faith that I do not flinch at anything the devil tries to do to me. Rather than give in to my flesh and let worry conquer me, help me to remember the assignment You've given to me and to remain committed to finishing my course on time! I pray this in Jesus' name!

***

ABOUT THE AUTHOR

Dr. Victoria Dunston is a native of the Charlotte, North Carolina area. She is the eldest of three siblings, a mother of three, and a grandmother of nine. Victoria received her Doctorate of Divinity from St. Thomas Christian College in Jacksonville, Florida, and is also a graduate of Gaston College located in Gastonia, North Carolina. She has written numerous books, including the remarkably successful *Hoodwinked, Duped, & Bamboozled!, 21 Days of Intimacy Book & Devotional,* and an intercessory prayer manual.

She is a serial entrepreneur, has several thriving businesses, and has recently started the Boss Lady Network, which is a network for women entrepreneurs. The network provides coaching, training, administrative assistance, and support.

Over the past thirteen years, Dr. Victoria has worked as an experienced management professional with a proven record of leadership in the nonprofit sector. She has extensive experience in education, women recovering from substance abuse advocacy, organizational partnerships, and is CEO and founder of N'Spired Training & Development Center. She has worked tirelessly for the past eighteen years to see the issues of school abandonment reduction, child advocacy, youth development, and nonprofit management advance in the City of Orlando and currently internationally. One of her proudest accomplishments is being the founder and principal of Victory Prep Christian Academy.

As a motivational speaker, Dr. Victoria touches issues such as the causes of breakdowns in relationships, and is in anticipation of writing self-help books that will target toxic relationships, "when helping you starts to hurt me," and overcoming the enabler syndrome. She has given presentations and speeches at all levels, from CEO/

Chairman meetings to colleges, universities, and high schools all the across the United States.

In addition, Dr. Victoria is a music recording artist, making appearances on the *Bobby Jones Gospel Show* and TBN, and has traveled and ministered abroad musically, speaking in countries in Europe (France, England, and Holland), the Islands (Jamaica and Bahamas), and South America (Honduras). She has enjoyed working for diverse, community-focused organizations and constructing strategic alliances with public and private organizations. In addition to all these other accomplishments, she also served as a pastor for over twelve years. As a "tent maker" for much of her life, Dr. Victoria always used her various occupations and roles in the marketplace to share her life-altering experiences.

Dr. Victoria Dunston is an extraordinarily honorable woman who has an authenticity with the aim of inspiration, which is why she was led by God to recently start a group called The Throne Room Company that focuses on mentoring and training those called to the apostolic and prophetic mandates in prayer, worship, and the prophetic. She was also a chosen recipient of the Dr. Martin Luther King Service Award and President Barak Obama Community Service Award, for continuing to make huge strides in the community by creating jobs and other opportunities for others to fulfill their dreams.

This book is her most precious writing and is inspired by several things she has had to walk through over the past five years. She knows what it means to have to "outlive" a sea of lies, misconceptions, and wrong judgments. It is not written to uncover the shortcomings of others, but to shed light on who you can become while walking through painful processes.

This book is designed to give you tools and biblical examples of people just like you and me, who have had to face and deal with the effects of accusation. It is hard. It can be heartbreaking, but the truth is, "No weapon formed against you shall *prosper*" (Isaiah 54:17 NKJV). You are not a victim—you are victorious; you were not just attacked—you were considered, and promotion is on the horizon.

Acknowledgments

This book is dedicated to the loving memory of my mother, Georgia Mae Norman. She was my inspiration and greatest support. In my memory, she demonstrated great strength and fought to live and to love. I learned from watching her that real strength comes from being determined to believe God concerning His Word.

I observed her going through many attacks, and yet she was still determined to live. Although there were times when she did not know how to handle situations, she remained

steadfast in her faith. I was with her for over fifty-six years. I saw the highs and lows of her life. I saw how life was unfair and very unkind to her, yet she refused to quit.

She also watched me walk through the many trials and adversities of life, and oftentimes took on my battles as her own. She wanted me to succeed. Every endeavor I attempted, she was standing right there, and I knew I had her support.

Mom, I survived the sea of lies and stand strong on the Word of God that no weapon formed against me will ever prosper. Even though you are not here to see me in my now, you can observe from heaven that God did not forget about me! I survived it, and I am rebuilding better and stronger.

Sticks and stones may break my bones, *but* words from God, spoken by me, are *a game changer!*

— Dr. Victoria

CPSIA information can be obtained
at www.ICGtesting.com
Printed in the USA
LVHW082123110821
695091LV00011B/326